NCO

OLYMPIAD WORKBOOK

5

NATIONAL CYBER OLYMPIAD

AF362202

01 Learning Objectives

02 Multiple Choice Questions

03 HOTS (Achievers Section)

04 Model Test Paper

05 Answer Keys and Solutions

06 OMR Answer Sheet

V&S PUBLISHERS

Published by:

V&S PUBLISHERS

F-2/16, Ansari road, Daryaganj, New Delhi-110002
☎ 23240026, 23240027 • *Fax:* 011-23240028
✉ info@vspublishers.com • 🌐 www.vspublishers.com

 **Online Brandstore: amazon.in/vspublishers**

Regional Office : Hyderabad
5-1-707/1, Brij Bhawan (Beside Central Bank of India Lane)
Bank Street, Koti, Hyderabad - 500 095
☎ 040-24737290
✉ vspublishershyd@gmail.com

Follow us on:   

BUY OUR BOOKS FROM: AMAZON FLIPKART

© **Copyright:** V&S PUBLISHERS
ISBN 978-81-978176-9-4
New Edition

DISCLAIMER

PUBLISHER'S NOTE

V&S Publishers has carved a significant niche in the publishing industry over the last decade, having successfully published more than 1000 titles across 9 languages spanning over 50 subject categories. Being known for the quality of content, we have built a reputation of excellence and reliability. We have consistently delivered **"Value & Substance"** to our readers, through a wide range of titles across a variety of genres covering school books, fiction and non-fiction that caters to different people from every section of the society.

The **Olympiad Guidebooks for classes 1-10** across all subjects, launched almost a decade ago, under the **GEN X Imprint**, became a go-to-source for the school students in no time, owing to their invaluable and substantive content written in a guidebook pattern,.

Having successfully sold a million copies of the same and in response to demand by both students as well as shopkeepers nationwide; we now present before you our newly launched **Olympiad Workbook Series**, designed for **classes 1-10 across 4 subjects**.

The workbooks are meticulously curated by a team of experienced educators, researchers and subject matter experts, edited by professionals and peer reviewed by teachers. The team has poured its efforts and expertise into creating a crisp and concise workbook which will help and guide the students to the path of success in Olympiad exams. The **MCQs** identified will not only help in scoring top marks in Olympiads but also inculcate a sense of deeper understanding of the subject, by way of solving **HOTS** and referring to complete solutions at the end of the book.

Here we present our new release– **OLYMPIAD WORKBOOK (NCO) CLASS–5** having following features:

☞ Based on the latest syllabi

☞ MCQs with comprehensive coverage of topics

☞ HOTS Questions liberally included

☞ A dedicated chapter on logical reasoning

☞ Model test paper for thorough practice

☞ Sample OMR sheet for real time simulation

We have made sure through our best efforts, that this workbook strictly follows the latest syllabi and patterns of the Olympiad Examination.

As **V&S Publishers** continuously strive to enhance the readability and maintain the credibility of our academic publications, we seek the support of our valuable readers in influencing and enriching the lives of future generations of students.

P.S. While every care has been taken to ensure the correctness of the content, if you come across any error, howsoever minor, do not hesitate to discuss with teachers while pointing that out to us in no uncertain terms.

We wish you all the best for your exams!

DISTINCTIVE FEATURES

01 — Learning Objectives

They list the whole chapter as subtopics, helping the teachers to guide children in a step-by-step manner.

02 — Multiple Choice Questions

MCQs act as an excellent learning aid, helping you to understand and work on your mistakes.

03 — HOTS (Achievers Section)

The High Order Thinking Questions aim to help the student to solve Application-based questions and gain practical understanding of the subject.

04 — Model Test Paper

Model test paper are provided at the end of each book, which help the student to test the knowledge which they have gained after thorough reading of all chapters.

05 — Answer Key

Detailed Answer Key along with explanations aid the pupil to indentify, understand the mistakes they make during the course of Olympiad preparation.

CONTENTS

FUNDAMENTALS OF COMPUTERS

LEARNING OBJECTIVES

➤ Hardware
➤ Output Devices
➤ Software
➤ Input Devices
➤ CPU Components

MULTIPLE CHOICE QUESTIONS

1. A mouse with a sphere that is moved for navigation instead of moving the whole mouse.
   (A) Zip Disk
   (B) Trackball
   (C) Optical Mouse
   (D) Keyboard

2. A device that emits computer audio audible to everyone
   (A) Speakers
   (B) Trackball
   (C) Printer
   (D) Magnetic Tape

3. A magnetic device using which the cursor is moved by touching with the fingers.
   (A) Light pen
   (B) Trackpad
   (C) Trackball
   (D) Touchpad

4. A device that converts soft copy to hard copy
   (A) Printer
   (B) Mouse
   (C) Magnetic Disk
   (D) Scanner

5. What is the common name for a video camera that streams video over the Internet?
   (A) iCaming
   (B) Netcam
   (C) Intercam
   (D) Webcam

6. Which of the following is NOT a type of flat-screen display?
   (A) LCD
   (B) LED
   (C) CRT
   (D) Plasma

7. Which of the following is NOT an impact printer?
   (A) Daisy Wheel
   (B) Drum
   (C) Chain
   (D) Thermal

8. What unit of measurement is used to measure digital camera image resolution?
   (A) Megabytes
   (B) Magahertz
   (C) Megatons
   (D) Megapix

9. Caps Lock, Num Lock and Scroll Lock are called ______.
   (A) Keyboard Shortcuts
   (B) Toggle Keys
   (C) Number Keys
   (D) Modifier Keys

10. A Dot matrix printer is an example of what type of printer?
    (A) Inkjet Printer
    (B) Laser Printer
    (C) Impact Printer
    (D) 3D Printer

11. What is dot pitch used to measure?
    (A) The sharpness of a monitor's display
    (B) The resolution of a printed document
    (C) The megapixel count of a digital camera
    (D) The shape of individual pixels on a screen

12. Which part instructs the ALU?
    (A) Memory
    (B) Control Unit
    (C) Keyboard
    (D) Monitor

13. A _________ is a peripheral device that allows a computer to connect and communicate with other computers.
    (A) ISP
    (B) Web browser
    (C) Telephone Lines
    (D) Modulator-demodulator

14. Motherboards, memory modules, and network interface cards are all types of
    (A) PCBs
    (B) CCDs
    (C) CPUs
    (D) VLBs

15. What is the purpose of UPS?
    (A) It ensures to connect power to the devices when the electricity goes out.
    (B) It balances the bandwidth of multiple network connections.
    (C) It allows single computer to work with multiple monitors.
    (D) It prevents unauthorized devices from accessing a wireless network.

16. "Power strip" is another name for which device?
    (A) Power Adaptor
    (B) Power Supply
    (C) Power Board
    (D) Fuse Box

17. What is the standard resolution of VGA display?
    (A) 1860 × 234 pixels
    (B) 640 × 480 pixels
    (C) 1024 × 768 pixels
    (D) 1920 × 1080 pixels

18. Which of the following is an example of an optical disc drive?
    (A) Tape Drive
    (B) DVD Drive
    (C) Internal SSD
    (D) External Hard Drive

19. What is the purpose of a CPU heat sink?
    (A) It blows cool air onto the processor.
    (B) It stores energy create by the processor to power the computer.
    (C) It dissipates heat from the processor.
    (D) It keeps the processor warm enough to function correctly.

20. Which of the following is the most recent type of hardware interface?
    (A) USB
    (B) Fire Wire
    (C) Thunderbolt
    (D) eSATA

HOTS (ACHIEVERS SECTION)

21. Identify the kind of program described below.
    - System designers use this program over wired electronic circuit to perform high-level operations.
    - Good example of it is "system boot program".
    - A computer needs this program every time it is switched ON and the computer must retain it even when it is switched OFF.
    (A) Mini Program
    (B) Demo Program
    (C) Micro Program
    (D) Major Program

22. Which of the following statements is incorrect about magnetic tapes?

(A) It is not suitable for storage of those data that we need to access randomly.

(B) There is no need to label magnetic tapes properly and logically to remember what data is on which tape.

(C) It should be stored in dust free environment.

(D) Both (A) and (B)

23. In a mainframe computer, numerous programs are loaded in a memory and its operating system runs those programs one by one and executes them simultaneously. This technique is called __________.

(A) Multitasking

(B) Multiprocessing

(C) Multithreading

(D) Multiuser

24. Main board and logic board are alternative names of which computer component?

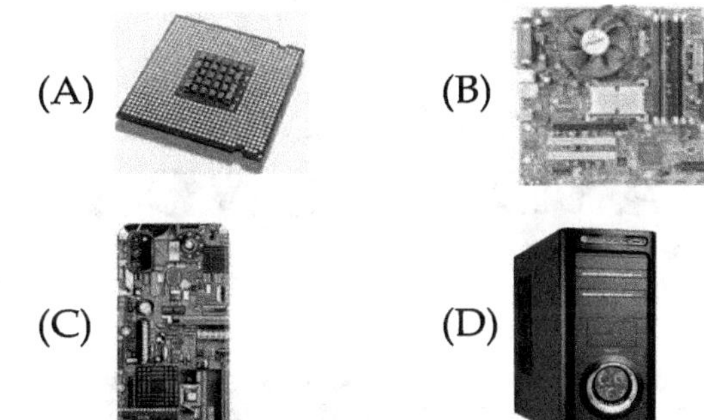

25. A CPU processes the data and instruction provided through the input devices and then passes the processed result to the output devices. Identify the device on which it is present.

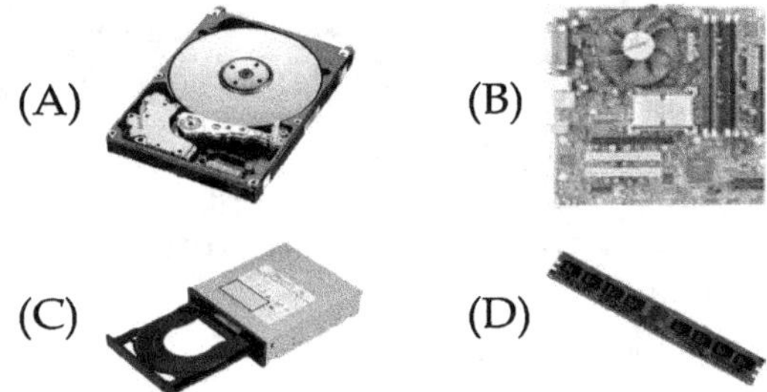

COMPUTER MEMORY-PRIMARY AND SECONDARY MEMORY 

LEARNING OBJECTIVES

➤ Primary Memory
➤ Secondary Memory
➤ Hard Disk

MULTIPLE CHOICE QUESTIONS

1. It is a magnetic disk storage medium sealed in a square plastic carrier lined with fabric that removes dust particles.
   (A) Floppy disk
   (B) Compact disc
   (C) Optical disc
   (D) Zip disk

2. A small plastic disc used for the storage of digital data, originally developed for audio system. What it is called?
   (A) Compact disc
   (B) Floppy disk
   (C) Optical disc
   (D) Zip disk

3. The storage capacity of a computer is called its _____.
   (A) Storage space
   (B) Stack
   (C) Pile
   (D) Memory

4. Internal memory is synonymous with which memory?
   (A) Primary
   (B) Secondary
   (C) Tertiary
   (D) None of these

5. What is the full form of ROM?
   (A) Random Only Memory
   (B) Read Only Memory
   (C) Random Order Memory
   (D) Read Order Memory

6. Which of the following is a type of internal memory?
   (A) RAM
   (B) ROM
   (C) Both (A) and (B)
   (D) None of these

7. Which is the built in memory of a computer?
   (A) RAM
   (B) ROM
   (C) Hard disk
   (D) Flash drive

8. Which memory is called read/write memory?
   (A) RAM
   (B) ROM
   (C) Hard disk
   (D) Flash drive

9. Which memory is a volatile memory?
   (A) RAM
   (B) ROM
   (C) Hard disk
   (D) Flash drive

10. The storage of data and instructions in ROM are _____.
   (A) Volatile
   (B) Erasable
   (C) Permanent
   (D) Changeable

11. What is the full form of PROM?
   (A) Processed Read Only Memory
   (B) Promoter Read Only Memory
   (C) Printable Read Only Memory
   (D) Programmable Read Only Memory

12. What is the full form of EEPROM?
   (A) Electronically Erasable Programmable Read Only Memory
   (B) Electrically Erasable Programmable Read Only Memory
   (C) Electronically Erasable Printable Read Only Memory
   (D) Electrically Erasable Printable Read Only Memory

13. Which of these is NOT a secondary memory?
   (A) Hard disk
   (B) Random Access Memory
   (C) Flash drive
   (D) CD-ROM

14. Which of the following is a dimension of floppy disk?
   (A) 3.5 inch
   (B) 5.25 inch
   (C) Both (A) and (B)
   (D) None of these

15. Hard disk is made up of a collection of disks known as _____.
   (A) Serials
   (B) Platters
   (C) Tracks
   (D) Bundles

16. Match the following:

Column-I	Column-II
(i) 1 Byte	(a) Secondary Memory
(ii) RAM	(b) 8 bits
(iii) PROM	(c) Ultraviolet light
(iv) EPROM	(d) Once programmer, cannot be erased
(v) Pen Drive	(e) Power Supply dependent

   (A) (i) – a, (ii) – e, (iii) – d, (iv) – c, (v) – b
   (B) (i) – b, (ii) – c, (iii) – e, (iv) – d, (v) – a
   (C) (i) – a, (ii) – b, (iii) – d, (iv) – c, (v) – e
   (D) (i) – b, (ii) – e, (iii) – d, (iv) – c, (v) – a

17. Which of the following is NOT a type of primary memory?
   (A) PROM
   (B) CD-ROM
   (C) EPROM
   (D) EEPORM

18. Which of them is another name of pen drive?
   (A) Flash drive
   (B) USB drive
   (C) Both (A) and (B)
   (D) None of these

19. It is the type of ROM, in which the recorded information can be erased by exposing it to ultraviolet light.
   (A) RAM
   (B) PROM
   (C) EEPROM
   (D) EPROM

20. 1 TB = _____.
   (A) 1024 KB
   (B) 1024 GB
   (C) 1024 MB
   (D) 1024 KB

21. Sheetal wrote a computer exam where she marked her answers by darkening circles on pre-printed sheets. Which of the following devices will be used to check her answer sheet?

(A) 

(B) 

(C) 

(D) 

22. If you want to edit and save your files over and over again in the same CD, which of the following type of CDs would you need to use?

(A) CD-WORM (B) CD-RW

(C) CD-ROM (D) CD-DOD

23. Arrange the following in decreasing order of their storage capacity CD-ROM, DVD, Blu-ray

(A) CD-ROM → DVD→ Blu-ray

(B) CD-ROM→ Blu-ray →DVD

(C) DVD → Blu-ray → CD-ROM

(D) Blu-ray → DVD → CD-ROM

24. SIMMs and DIMMs are different types of which computer component?

(A) 

(B) 

(C) 

(D) 

25. Identify the device shown here and select the statement which is CORRECT about it.

(A) It affects the number and size of programs that a system can run simultaneously.

(B) It is the main secondary storage found inside a computer.

(C) It is used to store and transfer data from one computer to another.

(D) It is attached with the CPU through USB port.

Darken Your Choice with HB Pencil

1.	Ⓐ Ⓑ Ⓒ Ⓓ	6.	Ⓐ Ⓑ Ⓒ Ⓓ	11.	Ⓐ Ⓑ Ⓒ Ⓓ	16.	Ⓐ Ⓑ Ⓒ Ⓓ	21.	Ⓐ Ⓑ Ⓒ Ⓓ
2.	Ⓐ Ⓑ Ⓒ Ⓓ	7.	Ⓐ Ⓑ Ⓒ Ⓓ	12.	Ⓐ Ⓑ Ⓒ Ⓓ	17.	Ⓐ Ⓑ Ⓒ Ⓓ	22.	Ⓐ Ⓑ Ⓒ Ⓓ
3.	Ⓐ Ⓑ Ⓒ Ⓓ	8.	Ⓐ Ⓑ Ⓒ Ⓓ	13.	Ⓐ Ⓑ Ⓒ Ⓓ	18.	Ⓐ Ⓑ Ⓒ Ⓓ	23.	Ⓐ Ⓑ Ⓒ Ⓓ
4.	Ⓐ Ⓑ Ⓒ Ⓓ	9.	Ⓐ Ⓑ Ⓒ Ⓓ	14.	Ⓐ Ⓑ Ⓒ Ⓓ	19.	Ⓐ Ⓑ Ⓒ Ⓓ	24.	Ⓐ Ⓑ Ⓒ Ⓓ
5.	Ⓐ Ⓑ Ⓒ Ⓓ	10.	Ⓐ Ⓑ Ⓒ Ⓓ	15.	Ⓐ Ⓑ Ⓒ Ⓓ	20.	Ⓐ Ⓑ Ⓒ Ⓓ	25.	Ⓐ Ⓑ Ⓒ Ⓓ

INTRODUCTION TO MULTIMEDIA

LEARNING OBJECTIVES

➤ Text
➤ Sound/Audio
➤ Animation
➤ Protoco
➤ Images
➤ Video

MULTIPLE CHOICE QUESTIONS

1. Multimedia is __________.
   (A) Picture
   (B) Sound
   (C) Animation
   (D) All of these

2. What is the most common way to discover a media?
   (A) By the name
   (B) By file location
   (C) By file extension
   (D) None of these

3. MP3 is an extension for __________.
   (A) Sound/Audio/Music file
   (B) Video file
   (C) Data files of pictures
   (D) Graphic file

4. __________ is a simulation of movement created by displaying a series of pictures.
   (A) Movie
   (B) Picture
   (C) Animation
   (D) Sound

5. Picture formats can be recognized by which extensions?
   (A) .gif
   (B) .jpg
   (C) Both (a) and (B)
   (D) None of these

6. The MP3 format is synonymous with __________.
   (A) MPGE
   (B) MPPP
   (C) MPEG
   (D) AU

7. What is the full form of MPEG?
   (A) Motion Pictures Experts Group
   (B) Moving Pictures Experts Group
   (C) Motion Pictures Expanding Group
   (D) Motion Page Expanding Group

8. Videos can be stored using the AVI format. What does AVI stand for?
   (A) Audio Video Interface
   (B) Audio Video Interleave
   (C) Audio Video Interaction
   (D) Audio Video Internet

9. What are the extensions of Windows Media files?
   (A) .asf
   (B) .asf
   (C) .wmv
   (D) All of these

10. .wmv stand for __________.
    (A) Windows Media Video
    (B) Windows Motion Verdict
    (C) Windows Media Version
    (D) Windows Motion Video

11. What is the default buffering time for windows media player?
    (A) 10 sec
    (B) 2 sec
    (C) 4 sec
    (D) 5 sec

12. What does JPEG stand for?
    (A) Joint Picture Expert Group
    (B) Joint Picture Enhancing Group
    (C) Joint Photographic Experts Group
    (D) Joint Photo Expert Graphic

13. A play queue is a __________ song listing that allows you to easily select and sort tracks.
    (A) Permanent
    (B) Stored
    (C) Temporary
    (D) Long

14. The __________ is a play queue.
    (A) List   (B) Library
    (C) Play list Editor   (D) None of these
15. An equalizer allows you to control the __________ of the songs you are playing.
    (A) Audio volumes
    (B) Audio frequencies
    (C) Audio extensions
    (D) Audio noise
16. The Quick Time format was developed by __________.
    (A) Intel   (B) Microsoft
    (C) Apple Inc   (D) HP
17. The Real Video format is developed by __________.
    (A) Microsoft   (B) Real Networks
    (C) Apple Inc   (D) HP
18. What is the extension of videos stored in Real Video format?
    (A) .rm   (B) .wm
    (C) Both (A) and (B)   (D) None of these
19. The tiny dots comprising a picture are called __________.
    (A) Images   (B) Pixels
    (C) Matter   (D) Points
20. .gif stand for __________.
    (A) Graphics Identification Format
    (B) Graphics Interchange Format
    (C) Graphic Identity File
    (D) Graphic Interface Format

HOTS (ACHIEVERS SECTION)

21. In the given image, face 1 and face 2 blends together in such a way that it distorts the first face to have the shape of second face and at the same time turning into another new face 3. What is this technique called?

Face 1   Face 2   Face 3

    (A) Rendering   (B) Sampling
    (C) Morphing   (D) Retarding
22. Resolution of XGA monitor is ______.
    (A) 1024 × 768   (B) 800 × 600
    (C) 640 × 480   (D) 320 × 200
23. Mrs. Kapoor wants to gift a digital album to her friend on her birthday. All the images are static and have lots of colour shading. Which of the following format is best suited for this purpose?
    (A) AUI   (B) JPEG
    (C) GIF   (D) Bitmap
24. In __________ streaming, there is no need to store data before delivering it, here data is processed quickly by buffering.
    (A) Batch-time   (B) Patch
    (C) Real-time   (D) Static
25. When audio and video segments of a multimedia files are interleaved together to reduce the number of records to store them, it is called as __________.
    (A) Scanning   (B) Flattening
    (C) Spotting   (D) Densing

―Darken Your Choice with HB Pencil―

1.	Ⓐ Ⓑ Ⓒ Ⓓ	6.	Ⓐ Ⓑ Ⓒ Ⓓ	11.	Ⓐ Ⓑ Ⓒ Ⓓ	16.	Ⓐ Ⓑ Ⓒ Ⓓ	21.	Ⓐ Ⓑ Ⓒ Ⓓ
2.	Ⓐ Ⓑ Ⓒ Ⓓ	7.	Ⓐ Ⓑ Ⓒ Ⓓ	12.	Ⓐ Ⓑ Ⓒ Ⓓ	17.	Ⓐ Ⓑ Ⓒ Ⓓ	22.	Ⓐ Ⓑ Ⓒ Ⓓ
3.	Ⓐ Ⓑ Ⓒ Ⓓ	8.	Ⓐ Ⓑ Ⓒ Ⓓ	13.	Ⓐ Ⓑ Ⓒ Ⓓ	18.	Ⓐ Ⓑ Ⓒ Ⓓ	23.	Ⓐ Ⓑ Ⓒ Ⓓ
4.	Ⓐ Ⓑ Ⓒ Ⓓ	9.	Ⓐ Ⓑ Ⓒ Ⓓ	14.	Ⓐ Ⓑ Ⓒ Ⓓ	19.	Ⓐ Ⓑ Ⓒ Ⓓ	24.	Ⓐ Ⓑ Ⓒ Ⓓ
5.	Ⓐ Ⓑ Ⓒ Ⓓ	10.	Ⓐ Ⓑ Ⓒ Ⓓ	15.	Ⓐ Ⓑ Ⓒ Ⓓ	20.	Ⓐ Ⓑ Ⓒ Ⓓ	25.	Ⓐ Ⓑ Ⓒ Ⓓ

WINDOWS 10

LEARNING OBJECTIVES

- ➤ HomeGroup
- ➤ Pinning any program
- ➤ Jump Lists
- ➤ Windows Search

MULTIPLE CHOICE QUESTIONS

1. _____ is a program that helps in viewing and managing files and folders.
   - (A) Windows Manager
   - (B) Windows Explorer
   - (C) File Handler
   - (D) Control Panel

2. In Windows, files are stored in locations called _____.
   - (A) Storage
   - (B) Programs
   - (C) Folders
   - (D) Stacks

3. What does the left pane in Windows Explorer display?
   - (A) Images
   - (B) Files
   - (C) Drives and Folders
   - (D) None of these

4. Where can you find all storage locations on a computer?
   - (A) 
   - (B) 
   - (C) 
   - (D) 

5. What is pinning?
   - (A) On the start button, you can right-click the icon to view recently used files in a jump list.
   - (B) Link to folder containing the items you see the most
   - (C) To easily access programs, you can attach, or pin a program icon directly to the taskbar or Start menu.
   - (D) The common center for configuring Windows settings

6. What is Windows Taskbar?
   - (A) Identifies the path for the currently open folder.
   - (B) The command center for configuring Windows settings.
   - (C) Software that controls the basic operations of your computer.
   - (D) Appears at the bottom of the screen and displays icons of programs that you can easily access.

7. _____ tell windows the type of a file and the program that would be used to open it.
   - (A) Folder names
   - (B) Drive names
   - (C) File extensions
   - (D) File names

8. What is address bar?
   (A) Software that control the basic operation of your computer.
   (B) Store the file you want to delete and operations your computer.
   (C) The main work area in Windows.
   (D) Identify the path for the currently open folder.

9. .wav is an extension used by _______ files.
   (A) Audio   (B) Video
   (C) Text   (D) Picture

10. What does DLL stand for?
   (A) Data Link List
   (B) Disk Link Library
   (C) Dynamic Link Library
   (D) None of these

11. How is information organized on a drive?
   (A) Files   (B) Folders
   (C) Sub-folders   (D) All of these

12. What characteristic of a file must be specified to save it?
   (A) File name   (B) File location
   (C) File extension (D) All of these

13. Which of the following is Windows application program?
   (A) Notepad
   (B) Windows Explorer
   (C) Paint
   (D) All of these

14. A set of routines that work closely with the hardware to support the transfer of information between elements of the system, such as memory disks and the monitor is called _______.
   (A) BIUS   (B) BIOS
   (C) BOIP   (D) None of these

15. The graphical system that manages what appears on the screen and provides graphics support for printers and other output device is called _______.
   (A) DGI   (B) IGD
   (C) GDI   (D) GUI

16. What is the use of the Control Panel?
   (A) Identifies the path for the currently open folder.
   (B) The command center for configuration Windows settings.
   (C) Used to close a window.
   (D) To easily access programs, you can attach, or pin a program icon drectly to the taskbar or Start menu.

17. Which of the following provides important messages about critical security and maintenance components on your computer, such as the firewall, antivirus protection and spyware protection?
   (A) Pointer
   (B) Jump List
   (C) Computer Folder
   (D) Action Center

18. In this area, you can check the time and date, adjust speaker volume and access other network or system features.
   (A) Notification area
   (B) Status bar
   (C) Action Center
   (D) Start button

19. A _______ is a "mini-menu" of performance tasks for an icon on the taskbar.
   (A) Gadget
   (B) Snap
   (C) Jump List
   (D) Pin task

20. Identify the icon given here.

   (A) Computer
   (B) Network
   (C) Windows Explorer
   (D) Recycle Bin

21. Raman has opened few programs on Windows 7 and is switching between them from time to time. Which of the following shortcut keys will let him cycle through the programs on the taskbar in the order they are accessed?
    (A) Alt + Tab + F4
    (B) ⊞ + Home
    (C) Alt + Shift + Esc
    (D) ⊞ + D

22. _____ is a set of routines that performs a variety of generalized operations such as sorting, searching, merging copying, printing and maintenance on data files.
    (A) File utilities
    (B) File organization
    (C) File management
    (D) FTP

23. Which of the following syntax should be typed in the search box of start menu to search picture files in any indexed format such as JPEG, GIF, Bitmap, PNG, as well as icons and shortcuts to image files?
    (A) Kind/pic   (B) Kind = pic
    (C) Kind//pic   (D) Kind: = pic

24. _____ is a Window utility program that locates and eliminates unnecessary fragments and rearranges files and unused disk space to optimize operations.
    (A) Disk Defragmenter
    (B) Restore
    (C) Disk Cleanup
    (D) Backup

25. File ___ shrinks the size of a file so it requires less storage space.
    (A) Compression
    (B) Defragmenting
    (C) Synthesizing
    (D) Scanning

Darken Your Choice with HB Pencil

1.	Ⓐ Ⓑ Ⓒ Ⓓ	6.	Ⓐ Ⓑ Ⓒ Ⓓ	11.	Ⓐ Ⓑ Ⓒ Ⓓ	16.	Ⓐ Ⓑ Ⓒ Ⓓ	21.	Ⓐ Ⓑ Ⓒ Ⓓ
2.	Ⓐ Ⓑ Ⓒ Ⓓ	7.	Ⓐ Ⓑ Ⓒ Ⓓ	12.	Ⓐ Ⓑ Ⓒ Ⓓ	17.	Ⓐ Ⓑ Ⓒ Ⓓ	22.	Ⓐ Ⓑ Ⓒ Ⓓ
3.	Ⓐ Ⓑ Ⓒ Ⓓ	8.	Ⓐ Ⓑ Ⓒ Ⓓ	13.	Ⓐ Ⓑ Ⓒ Ⓓ	18.	Ⓐ Ⓑ Ⓒ Ⓓ	23.	Ⓐ Ⓑ Ⓒ Ⓓ
4.	Ⓐ Ⓑ Ⓒ Ⓓ	9.	Ⓐ Ⓑ Ⓒ Ⓓ	14.	Ⓐ Ⓑ Ⓒ Ⓓ	19.	Ⓐ Ⓑ Ⓒ Ⓓ	24.	Ⓐ Ⓑ Ⓒ Ⓓ
5.	Ⓐ Ⓑ Ⓒ Ⓓ	10.	Ⓐ Ⓑ Ⓒ Ⓓ	15.	Ⓐ Ⓑ Ⓒ Ⓓ	20.	Ⓐ Ⓑ Ⓒ Ⓓ	25.	Ⓐ Ⓑ Ⓒ Ⓓ

MS PAINT

LEARNING OBJECTIVES

- ➤ Opening a Paint Window
- ➤ Drawing Different Shapes
- ➤ Quick Access Toolbar
- ➤ Drawing Different Lines
- ➤ Adding Colour to an Image

MULTIPLE CHOICE QUESTIONS

Direction (1-4): Look at the bar on MS-Paint window and answer the following questions.

`+ 95, 420px    25 × 26px    768 × 480px    Size: 18.6KB    100%    ─────`

1. The image shown here is of ______.
   - (A) Status Bar
   - (B) Menu RIBBON
   - (C) Quick Access Toolbar
   - (D) Title Bar

2. What is 768 × 480 px shown in the image?
   - (A) Dimension of the drawing area.
   - (B) Dimension of the selected area of a drawing.
   - (C) Dimension of the selection tool.
   - (D) All of these

3. What is 25 × 26 shown in the image?
   - (A) Dimension of the drawing area
   - (B) Dimension of the selected area of a drawing.
   - (C) Dimension of the selection tool.
   - (D) All of these

4. In 768 × 480 px, ______ px is the length and ______ px is the breath respectively.
   - (A) 768, 480
   - (B) 480, 768
   - (C) 768, 768
   - (D) 480, 480

5. To change the unit to centimeter, you should go to the ______.
   - (A) View tab of the Ribbon
   - (B) Properties dialog in the Paint menu
   - (C) Home tab of the Ribbon
   - (D) Double click on the status bar

6. How do you hide the status bar?
   - (A) Uncheck "Status Bar" from the view tab of the Ribbon.
   - (B) Click "Hide Status Bar" in the Paint menu.
   - (C) Uncheck "Status Bar" from the Home tab of the Ribbon.
   - (D) Double click on the status bar.

7. Which shortcut should you use to view the drawing in full screen?
   - (A) F1
   - (B) F2
   - (C) F3
   - (D) F11

8. The ___ tool can be used to pick colors that you have already used in an image.
   - (A) Full Colors
   - (B) Eraser
   - (C) Color picker
   - (D) Brush

9. Observe the given image.

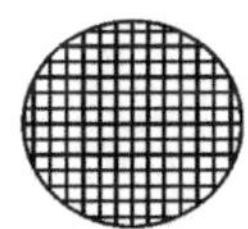

The third row of color boxes shows:
(A) Recently used colors
(B) Color which you use and are not available in the default palette.
(C) Colors that are used for background.
(D) None of these

10. The _____ tool is used to position and enter text in your drawing.
(A) ⟨image⟩   (B) **A**
(C) ⟨image⟩   (D) ⟨image⟩

11. What is the shortcut key to undo a change in the drawing?
(A) Ctrl + A   (B) Ctrl + X
(C) Ctrl + U   (D) Ctrl + Z

12. The drawing you create in MS Paint can be saved as_____.
(A) JPEG, PNG   (B) GIF, TIFF
(C) BMP   (D) All of these

13. Which keys will help you to select the whole page?
(A) Ctrl + C   (B) Ctrl + Z
(C) Ctrl + V   (D) Ctrl + A

14. Which of the following is NOT a valid option to rotate an image?
(A) Rotate left 90°
(B) Rotate right 90°
(C) Rotate 180°
(D) Rotate 270°

15. Which of the following can create an effect that can be used in making an illusion of 3D perspective?
(A) Skew   (B) Flip
(C) Rotate   (D) Stretch

16. Which of these image properties can you change using image properties dialog box?
(A) Units   (B) Colors
(C) Dimension   (D) All of these

17. The shortcut to view image Properties dialog box is_____.
(A) Ctrl + E   (B) Ctrl + A
(B) Ctrl + Z   (D) Ctrl + F

18. This picture shows a grid on the circle. How is the grid created?

(A) Enable Gridlines in the File of the ribbon.
(B) Use the line tool to create the grid.
(C) Use the rectangle tool to create the grid.
(D) Enable Gridlines in the view tab of the ribbon.

20. How do you transform the image in Figure 1 to the one given in Figure 2?

Figure 1   Figure 2
(A) Rotate left 90°
(B) Rotate 180°
(C) Rotate right 90°
(D) Flip vertical

21. To save a drawing in one of the available formats (png, jpeg, bmp, gif and other possible file types), go to Paint button and select ____________.

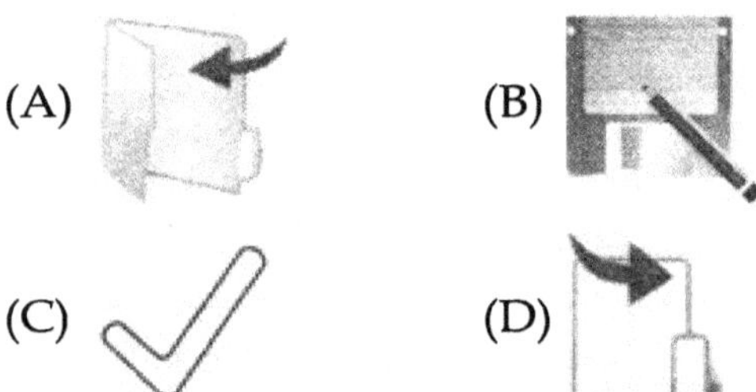

(A) (B) (C) (D)

22. Which command should you use to bring a Zoomed in or a Zoomed Out image to its original size?

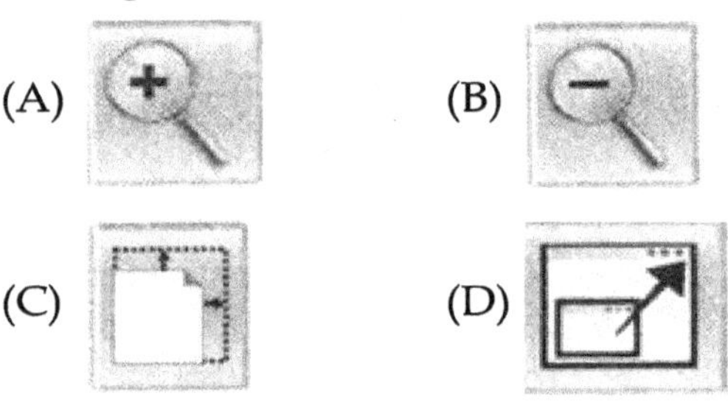

(A) (B) (C) (D)

23. What is the function of this tool in MS Paint?

(A) Draws a thin free form line. Used to draw objects just as you would with a pencil.

(B) Enables you to draw a text box to add typed words to an image.

(C) Fills an area with color.

(D) Picks up a color from one area of an image to use with a drawing tool.

24. You can set the drawing size of Paint in the computer like choosing the size of paper to use. To set the drawing size, what are the steps to follow?

(A) Ctrl + X

(B) Ctrl + H

(C) Image Menu | Attributes

(D) Image Menu | Flip/Rotate

	A B C D		A B C D		A B C D		A B C D		A B C D
1.	Ⓐ Ⓑ Ⓒ Ⓓ	6.	Ⓐ Ⓑ Ⓒ Ⓓ	11.	Ⓐ Ⓑ Ⓒ Ⓓ	16.	Ⓐ Ⓑ Ⓒ Ⓓ	21.	Ⓐ Ⓑ Ⓒ Ⓓ
2.	Ⓐ Ⓑ Ⓒ Ⓓ	7.	Ⓐ Ⓑ Ⓒ Ⓓ	12.	Ⓐ Ⓑ Ⓒ Ⓓ	17.	Ⓐ Ⓑ Ⓒ Ⓓ	22.	Ⓐ Ⓑ Ⓒ Ⓓ
3.	Ⓐ Ⓑ Ⓒ Ⓓ	8.	Ⓐ Ⓑ Ⓒ Ⓓ	13.	Ⓐ Ⓑ Ⓒ Ⓓ	18.	Ⓐ Ⓑ Ⓒ Ⓓ	23.	Ⓐ Ⓑ Ⓒ Ⓓ
4.	Ⓐ Ⓑ Ⓒ Ⓓ	9.	Ⓐ Ⓑ Ⓒ Ⓓ	14.	Ⓐ Ⓑ Ⓒ Ⓓ	19.	Ⓐ Ⓑ Ⓒ Ⓓ	24.	Ⓐ Ⓑ Ⓒ Ⓓ
5.	Ⓐ Ⓑ Ⓒ Ⓓ	10.	Ⓐ Ⓑ Ⓒ Ⓓ	15.	Ⓐ Ⓑ Ⓒ Ⓓ	20.	Ⓐ Ⓑ Ⓒ Ⓓ		

MS WORD

LEARNING OBJECTIVES

➤ Creating a New Document
➤ Bold, Underline and Italic Options
➤ Cut and Paste Options
➤ Shortcut Keys

MULTIPLE CHOICE QUESTIONS

1. Which of the following is NOT a valid version of MS Office?
   (A) Office Vista
   (B) Office XP
   (C) Office 2007
   (D) Office 2010

2. Pressing F8 key three times selects_____.
   (A) A word
   (B) A sentence
   (C) A paragraph
   (D) The Entire document

3. What does the key F12 display?
   (A) Save dialog box
   (B) Open dialog box
   (C) Close dialog box
   (D) Save As dialog box

4. What is the use of the ▣ button just above the vertical scroll bar?
   (A) To show and hide the Ribbon
   (B) To show and hide the scroll bars
   (C) To show and hide the Ruler.
   (D) To show and hide the Quick Access Toolbar.

5. What is the default font size of a new Word document based on Normal template?
   (A) 10pt
   (B) 11pt
   (C) 12pt
   (D) 8pt

6. Which of the following are/were Word processors?
   (A) Word Star
   (B) Word Perfect
   (C) Microsoft Write
   (D) All of these

7. Which option places the selected text slightly below the line of normal printed text?
   (A) Subscript
   (B) Superscript
   (C) Small front
   (D) Small caps

8. Match the following.

Column - I	Column - II
(i) Ctrl + F	(a) Replace
(ii) Ctrl + H	(b) Go to
(iii) Ctrl + C	(c) Bold
(iv) Ctrl + B	(d) Find

   (A) (i)–(d), (ii)–(a), (iii)–(b), (iv)–(c)
   (B) (i)–(a), (ii)–(b), (iii)–(c), (iv)–(d)
   (C) (i)–(d), (ii)–(c), (iii)–(a), (iv)–(b)
   (D) (i)–(a), (ii)–(d), (iii)–(b), (iv)–(c)

9. What does a ruler show?
   (A) Page width
   (B) Position of tabs, column, etc.
   (C) Length of the document
   (D) All of these

10. Which of the following is NOT a valid shortcut for setting the line spacing between lines of text?

(A) Ctrl + [! / 1]   (B) Ctrl + [@ / 2]

(C) Ctrl + [# / 3]   (D) None of these

11. ¶ is used to_____.
    (A) Create a new paragraph
    (B) Display or hide symbols for characters like spaces and tabs
    (C) Display or hide the title bar
    (D) Display or hide spelling and grammar errors

12. What are margins?
    (A) The amount of space between the text and the edge of the page on all four sides.
    (B) The amount of space on top.
    (C) The amount of space on sides.
    (D) The amount of space at bottom.

13. Match the following.

Column - I	Column - II
(i)	(a) Increase Indent
(ii)	(b) Align text to the right
(iii) x^2	(c) Start a bulleted list
(iv)	(d) Create small letters above the line of text
(v)	(e) Center text

(A) (i)–(a), (ii)–(e), (iii)–(d), (iv)–(b), (v)–(c)
(B) (i)–(c), (ii)–(b), (iii)–(d), (iv)–(e), (v)–(a)
(C) (i)–(c), (ii)–(b), (iii)–(a), (iv)–(e), (v)–(d)
(D) (i)–(c), (ii)–(e), (iii)–(d), (iv)–(b), (v)–(a)

14. Match the following.

Column - I	Column - II
(i) Ctrl + A	(a) Paste
(ii) Red Wavy	(b) Change Case lines
(iii)	(c) Synonyms and Antonyms
(iv) Aa	(d) Selects the entire document
(v) Thesaurus	(e) Spelling Mistakes

(A) (i)–(d), (ii)–(c), (iii)–(b), (iv)–(a), (v)–(e)
(B) (i)–(d), (ii)–(e), (iii)–(b), (iv)–(a), (v)–(c)
(C) (i)–(d), (ii)–(e), (iii)–(a), (iv)–(b), (v)–(c)
(D) (i)–(a), (ii)–(d), (iii)–(b), (iv)–(c), (v)–(e)

15. Which of the following can be used to set the size of a page?
    (A)
    (B)
    (C)
    (D)

16. How many column does a word document have by default?
    (A) One   (B) Two
    (C) Three   (D) Four

17. What is the shortcut to set the line spacing to 1.5?

    (A) Ctrl + [! / 1]

    (B) Ctrl + [@ / 2]

    (C) Ctrl + [# / 3]

    (D) Ctrl + [% / 5]

18. If I want 3 sets of copies of a document, what option should I select to get the first set complete of the whole document?
    (A) Numbers of copies
    (B) Collate
    (C) Scale
    (D) Pages

19. From the Print Menu you can do all the following except _____.
    (A) Print multiple copies
    (B) Preview the document
    (C) Change the document style
    (D) Adjust the page margins

20. Times New Roman, Comic Sans and Calibri are _____.
    (A) Fonts   (B) Styles
    (C) Text patterns   (D) Font sizes

21. The Styles task pane of MS Word 2010 is shown here. Styles have three kinds of icons next to them: ¶, a, ¶a. Which of the following statements is incorrect about ¶a icon?

    (A) It can be used either as character style or a paragraph style.

    (B) It cannot be applied only to a part of the paragraph.

    (C) It can be applied to the entire paragraph as well as to a part of the paragraph.

    (D) Both (A) and (B)

22. Find the odd one out in context to MS Word 2010.

    (A) A (B) abc

    (C) x^2 (D) ¶

23. Suppose you want to type a symbol ∞ (infinity) in MS Word 2010 document, which of the following steps is correct?

    (A) File → Options → Proofing → AutoCorrect Options → Math AutoCorrect

    (B) Home → AutoCorrect Options → Math AutoCorrect

    (C) Insert → Shapes → Math AutoCorrect

    (D) View → Options → PROOFING → autocorrect

24. Word has a list of predefined typing, spelling, capitalization, and grammar errors that ____________ can detect and correct.

    (A) AutoEntry

    (B) AutoCorrect

    (C) AutoAdd

    (D) AutoSpell

25. After typing header text, how can you quickly enter footer text?

    (A) Press Page-Down key and type the text for footer

    (B) Click on Switch between Heeder & Footer then type the text

    (C) Both of these

    (D) None of these

Darken Your Choice with HB Pencil

1.	Ⓐ Ⓑ Ⓒ Ⓓ	6.	Ⓐ Ⓑ Ⓒ Ⓓ	11.	Ⓐ Ⓑ Ⓒ Ⓓ	16.	Ⓐ Ⓑ Ⓒ Ⓓ	21.	Ⓐ Ⓑ Ⓒ Ⓓ
2.	Ⓐ Ⓑ Ⓒ Ⓓ	7.	Ⓐ Ⓑ Ⓒ Ⓓ	12.	Ⓐ Ⓑ Ⓒ Ⓓ	17.	Ⓐ Ⓑ Ⓒ Ⓓ	22.	Ⓐ Ⓑ Ⓒ Ⓓ
3.	Ⓐ Ⓑ Ⓒ Ⓓ	8.	Ⓐ Ⓑ Ⓒ Ⓓ	13.	Ⓐ Ⓑ Ⓒ Ⓓ	18.	Ⓐ Ⓑ Ⓒ Ⓓ	23.	Ⓐ Ⓑ Ⓒ Ⓓ
4.	Ⓐ Ⓑ Ⓒ Ⓓ	9.	Ⓐ Ⓑ Ⓒ Ⓓ	14.	Ⓐ Ⓑ Ⓒ Ⓓ	19.	Ⓐ Ⓑ Ⓒ Ⓓ	24.	Ⓐ Ⓑ Ⓒ Ⓓ
5.	Ⓐ Ⓑ Ⓒ Ⓓ	10.	Ⓐ Ⓑ Ⓒ Ⓓ	15.	Ⓐ Ⓑ Ⓒ Ⓓ	20.	Ⓐ Ⓑ Ⓒ Ⓓ	25.	Ⓐ Ⓑ Ⓒ Ⓓ

MS POWERPOINT

LEARNING OBJECTIVES

➤ Steps to Create a New Document
➤ Different Views
➤ Keyboard Shortcuts

MULTIPLE CHOICE QUESTIONS

Direction (1–4): View the PowerPoint window given below and answer the following questions.

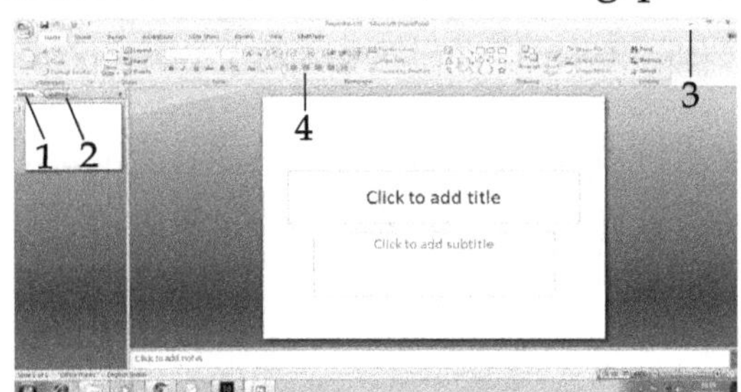

1. Area 1 displays the Slides tab. The Slides tab is used to _____.
   (A) Add and Delete slides
   (B) Duplicate slides
   (C) Rearrange slides
   (D) All of these

2. Area 2 displays the Outline tab. The outline tab is used for _____.
   (A) The text content of each slides
   (B) The presentation outline
   (C) The outline of the slide with images and text
   (D) All of these

3. Button 3 is used to _____.
   (A) Draw shape
   (B) Display scroll bar

   (C) Minimize the Ribbon
   (D) Display title bar

4. Button 4 is used to _____.
   (A) Split   (B) Justify
   (C) Align center   (D) Align left

5. A presentation is the collection of _____ arranged in a sequential manner.
   (A) Data   (B) Disks
   (C) Slides   (D) Documents

6. A _____ presentation is used to create slides with our own imagination.
   (A) Default   (B) Blank
   (C) Normal   (D) Basic

7. What is the shortcut key to create new presentation?
   (A) Ctrl + X   (B) Ctrl + N
   (C) Ctrl + A   (D) Ctrl + P

8. When you create a new presentation, the first slide will be the _____.
   (A) Blank slide   (B) Title slide
   (C) First slide   (D) Last slide

9. Which view displays the slides only with the buttons at the bottom?
   (A) Play slide show
   (B) Reading View

OLYMPIAD WORKBOOK (NCO) CLASS– 5

(C) Slide Sorter View

(D) Normal View

10. A new presentation always starts in the _______.
    (A) Normal View
    (B) Outline View
    (C) Slide Sorter View
    (D) Slide show

11. Which of the following is NOT a view in MS PowerPoint?
    (A) Zoomed View
    (B) Normal View
    (C) Slide Sorter View
    (D) Reading View

12. Which view displays smaller versions of all the slides in the presentation?
    (A) Slide View
    (B) Outline View
    (C) Slide Sorter View
    (D) Slide Show

13. Which of the following views displays the current slide and a text box for adding notes?
    (A) Slide Sorter View
    (B) Slide Show
    (C) Notes Page View
    (D) Outline View

14. In a normal view presentation, window is divided into _______ parts.
    (A) 1   (B) 2
    (C) 3   (D) 4

15. A presentation can contain which of the following objects?
    (A) Graphics
    (B) Movies
    (C) Sounds
    (D) All of these

16. To change the layout of a slide, you should _______.
    (A) Right click on the slide, click Layout then select the layout you want
    (B) Click Layout in the slides group of Insert tab
    (C) Click Layout in the slides group of the Home tab of the Ribbon
    (D) Both (A) and (B)

17. Which of the following should you use if you want to make changes to every slide in your presentation including ones added later to the presentation?
    (A) The Slide Layout option
    (B) Add a slide option
    (C) Outline View
    (D) Slide Master View

18. Which type of fonts are best suited for titles and headlines?
    (A) Serif fonts
    (B) Sans serif fonts
    (C) Text fonts
    (D) Picture fonts

19. (?) is used to _______
    (A) Close the presentation
    (B) Minimize the Ribbon
    (C) Provide Help
    (D) Close Power Point

20. To create videos, CD or handouts for your presentation, you should click on _______ in the Backstage view
    (A) Save As
    (B) Save and Send
    (C) Save
    (D) Options

21. Which of the following AutoFit behavior lets the added text overflow at the bottom of the text box when Wrap Text is ON in MS PowerPoint?
    (A) Do not Autofit
    (B) Shrink Text on Overflow
    (C) Resize Shape to Fit Text
    (D) All of these

22. Which of the following steps is incorrect to turn grid lines ON or OF in MS PowerPoint?
    (A) Press Shift + F9
    (B) Insert tab → Show group → Select or deselect the Grid lines check box
    (C) Home → Drawing → Arrange → Align → View Grid lines
    (D) Both (A) and (B)

23. In MS PowerPoint presentations, the designs regulate the layout and formatting for the slide. These are commonly known as:
    (A) Blueprints   (B) Placeholders
    (C) Templates   (D) Design Plates

24. The Handout Master consists of place-holders for all of these except the:
    (A) Title   (B) Slide number
    (C) Header   (D) Footer

25. Which of these PowerPoint features would allow any user to create a given simple presentation quicker?
    (A) Animations
    (B) Chart Wizard
    (C) Transition Wizard
    (D) AutoContent Wizard

Darken Your Choice with HB Pencil

1.	Ⓐ Ⓑ Ⓒ Ⓓ	6.	Ⓐ Ⓑ Ⓒ Ⓓ	11.	Ⓐ Ⓑ Ⓒ Ⓓ	16.	Ⓐ Ⓑ Ⓒ Ⓓ	21.	Ⓐ Ⓑ Ⓒ Ⓓ
2.	Ⓐ Ⓑ Ⓒ Ⓓ	7.	Ⓐ Ⓑ Ⓒ Ⓓ	12.	Ⓐ Ⓑ Ⓒ Ⓓ	17.	Ⓐ Ⓑ Ⓒ Ⓓ	22.	Ⓐ Ⓑ Ⓒ Ⓓ
3.	Ⓐ Ⓑ Ⓒ Ⓓ	8.	Ⓐ Ⓑ Ⓒ Ⓓ	13.	Ⓐ Ⓑ Ⓒ Ⓓ	18.	Ⓐ Ⓑ Ⓒ Ⓓ	23.	Ⓐ Ⓑ Ⓒ Ⓓ
4.	Ⓐ Ⓑ Ⓒ Ⓓ	9.	Ⓐ Ⓑ Ⓒ Ⓓ	14.	Ⓐ Ⓑ Ⓒ Ⓓ	19.	Ⓐ Ⓑ Ⓒ Ⓓ	24.	Ⓐ Ⓑ Ⓒ Ⓓ
5.	Ⓐ Ⓑ Ⓒ Ⓓ	10.	Ⓐ Ⓑ Ⓒ Ⓓ	15.	Ⓐ Ⓑ Ⓒ Ⓓ	20.	Ⓐ Ⓑ Ⓒ Ⓓ	25.	Ⓐ Ⓑ Ⓒ Ⓓ

INTERNET

LEARNING OBJECTIVES

- ➤ World Wide Web
- ➤ Web Browser
- ➤ Home and Tools Options
- ➤ Favorites, Feeds and History

MULTIPLE CHOICE QUESTIONS

1. The tools which help us to find information on the internet is called __________.
   - (A) Find engine
   - (B) Search engine
   - (C) Search pot
   - (D) Find station

2. Search engines search for websites based on ______.
   - (A) File
   - (B) Information
   - (C) Keywords
   - (D) Data

3. What is an advantage of e-mail?
   - (A) Speedy message spending process
   - (B) Can be used to multiple people at the same time
   - (C) Variety of media that can be sent
   - (D) All of these

4. How many parts does an e-mail address have?
   - (A) 2
   - (B) 1
   - (C) 3
   - (D) 4

5. Which of the following are the parts of an e-mail?
   - (A) Username
   - (B) @
   - (C) Host server name
   - (D) All of these

6. The domain name "org" is derived from __________.
   - (A) Organization
   - (B) Orbit
   - (C) Non-profit organization
   - (D) None of these

7. Application through which chatting can be done is called ________.
   - (A) Chat box
   - (B) Chat messenger
   - (C) Instant messenger
   - (D) Instant chat

8. Which of the following is NOT an Instant Messenger?
   - (A) skype
   - (B) talk
   - (C) icq
   - (D) Piriform

9. What can you search in a search engine?
   - (A) Articles, Stories and News
   - (B) Images and Pictures
   - (C) Games, Videos and Software
   - (D) All of these

10. Where do you type the URL in a browser?
    (A) Title bar
    (B) Scroll bar
    (C) Address bar
    (D) None of these

11. If you want to send e-mail to more than one person, you can type multiple e-mail addresses separated by __________
    (A) Colon   (B) Comma
    (C) Hyphen   (D) Slash

12. When chatting publicly, what should you NOT do?
    (A) Talk to strangers
    (B) Give your personal information
    (C) Reveal your identities
    (D) All of these

13. __________ is a software that is installed on a PC to take partial control over the user's interaction without user consent.
    (A) Docware
    (B) Spyware
    (C) Softspy
    (D) Spy

14. Obtaining unauthorized access to other systems in a network is called __________.
    (A) Access
    (B) Stealing
    (C) Forging
    (D) Hacking

15. How can you get rid of Pop-ups?
    (A) Pop up remover
    (B) Pop up saver
    (C) Pop up blocker
    (D) None of these

16. __________ is a system that prevents unauthorized use and access to your computer.
    (A) Protect
    (B) Firewall
    (C) Healwall
    (D) Heal

17. __________ program are used to remove spyware.
    (A) Adware
    (B) Pop up blocker
    (C) Firewall
    (D) Anti Spyware

18. What company devolved the Chrome web browser?

    (A) 

    (B) 

    (C) Google

    (D) 

19. What language is also known as the language of the web?
    (A) Java
    (B) C++
    (C) XML
    (D) HTML

20. What is the difference between Cc and Bcc in an e-mail?
    (A) Bcc supports attachments, while Cc does not.
    (B) Cc data is sent unencrypted, while Bcc is sent over a secure connection.
    (C) Bcc hides the sender's e-mail address, while Cc does not.
    (D) Bcc hides all of the recipient e-mail addresses, while Cc does not

21. Servers are computers that provide resources to other computers connected to a
    (A) Client
    (B) Mainframe
    (C) Supercomputer
    (D) Network

22. A program that is used to view websites is called a
    (A) Browser
    (B) Web viewer
    (C) Spreadsheet
    (D) Word processor

23. Which of the following is not a type of broadband internet connection?
    (A) Satellite (B) DSL
    (C) Dial up (D) Cable

24. A typical modern computer uses
    (A) Valves
    (B) LSI chips
    (C) Vacuum tubes
    (D) All of these

25. What is the term for unsolicited Email?
    (A) Spam (B) Backbone
    (C) Usenet (D) News group

—Darken Your Choice with HB Pencil—

1. Ⓐ Ⓑ Ⓒ Ⓓ	6. Ⓐ Ⓑ Ⓒ Ⓓ	11. Ⓐ Ⓑ Ⓒ Ⓓ	16. Ⓐ Ⓑ Ⓒ Ⓓ	21. Ⓐ Ⓑ Ⓒ Ⓓ
2. Ⓐ Ⓑ Ⓒ Ⓓ	7. Ⓐ Ⓑ Ⓒ Ⓓ	12. Ⓐ Ⓑ Ⓒ Ⓓ	17. Ⓐ Ⓑ Ⓒ Ⓓ	22. Ⓐ Ⓑ Ⓒ Ⓓ
3. Ⓐ Ⓑ Ⓒ Ⓓ	8. Ⓐ Ⓑ Ⓒ Ⓓ	13. Ⓐ Ⓑ Ⓒ Ⓓ	18. Ⓐ Ⓑ Ⓒ Ⓓ	23. Ⓐ Ⓑ Ⓒ Ⓓ
4. Ⓐ Ⓑ Ⓒ Ⓓ	9. Ⓐ Ⓑ Ⓒ Ⓓ	14. Ⓐ Ⓑ Ⓒ Ⓓ	19. Ⓐ Ⓑ Ⓒ Ⓓ	24. Ⓐ Ⓑ Ⓒ Ⓓ
5. Ⓐ Ⓑ Ⓒ Ⓓ	10. Ⓐ Ⓑ Ⓒ Ⓓ	15. Ⓐ Ⓑ Ⓒ Ⓓ	20. Ⓐ Ⓑ Ⓒ Ⓓ	25. Ⓐ Ⓑ Ⓒ Ⓓ

COMPUTER NETWORK

LEARNING OBJECTIVES

➤ LAN
➤ Intranet
➤ Network Interface Cards
➤ IP Addressing
➤ WAN
➤ MAN

MULTIPLE CHOICE QUESTIONS

1. A computer network is ______.
   (A) A collection of hardware components and computers
   (B) Computers which are connected to each other
   (C) Computers which share resources and information
   (D) All of these

2. A device or a system connected to a network is also called ______ .
   (A) Branch   (B) Leaf
   (C) Node   (D) Block

3. What is the benefit of networking?
   (A) Sharing files and data among connected computers.
   (B) Easy access to all resources like internet and printers over the network.
   (C) Earlier and faster backup of valuable data
   (D) All of these

4. Which of the following is a networking device?
   (A) Gateway
   (B) Router
   (C) Firewall
   (D) All of these

5. A device that encodes digital computer signals into anolog telephone signals and vice versa.
   (A) ISP
   (B) Web browser
   (C) Telephone Line
   (D) Modem

6. When computers in a computer laboratory in a school are connected, then such a connection of computers is called ______.
   (A) Internet
   (B) Local Area Network
   (C) Wide Area Network
   (D) Metropolitan Area Network

7. What does a protocol define in a network?
   (A) It defines what data is communicated.
   (B) It defines how data is communicated.
   (C) It defines when data is communicated.
   (D) All of these

8. Which of the following device is NOT essential to connect to the internet?
   (A) Modem
   (B) ISP
   (C) Telephone Line
   (D) Web Camera

9. What unit of measurement was used to describe dial-up modem speeds?
   (A) Kbps   (B) Gbps
   (C) KHz   (D) GHz

10. While browsing the internet, when you get the message "Web page cannot be displayed", what should you do?
    (A) Close the Browser
    (B) Click on the Favorite button
    (C) Click on the Stop button
    (D) Click on the Refresh button

11. What is the use of Ping command?
    (A) To test if the device on a network is reachable or not
    (B) To test a computer fault
    (C) To test a fault in the power supply
    (D) To test the quality of a painter

12. What is firewall in a network?
    (A) It is the physical boundary of a network.
    (B) A network operating system
    (C) A system preventing unauthorized access to a network
    (D) It is a web browsing software.

13. Radio waves and microwaves are used in which of the following communications?
    (A) Voice over
    (B) IP Telephony
    (C) Wireless
    (D) Office

14. A large number of computers in a wide geographical area can be efficiently connected by _____.
    (A) Cables
    (B) Magnetic rays
    (C) Twisted pair lines
    (D) Communication Satellites

15. A wireless network is also known as _____.
    (A) Wi-Fi network
    (B) Internet
    (C) Intranet
    (D) None of these

16. What protocol sends encrypted data over the Internet?
    (A) HTTP
    (B) SSL
    (C) SMPT
    (D) FTP

17. Which of the following statements is NOT netiquette?
    (A) You should tell your parents right away if you come across any information that make you feel uncomfortable.
    (B) Send anyone your picture or share any other personal information on the Internet without first consulting your parents.
    (C) Do not respond to any messages that in anyway make you feel uncomfortable.
    (D) Always talk to your parents so that together you can set up rules for going online.

18. A company that provides Internet access to a large number of users is called _____.
    (A) Website   (B) Web Host
    (C) ISP   (D) Web Server

19. A _____ is a computer program that browses the World Wide Web website that helps methodical and automated manner to create an information based on websites that help search engines in providing faster results to queries.
    (A) Web crawler   (B) Website
    (C) Windows   (D) Wallpaper

20. What is the search engine that searches multiple search engines called?
    (A) Metasearch Engine
    (B) Universal Search Engine
    (C) Search Portal
    (D) Search Station

21. 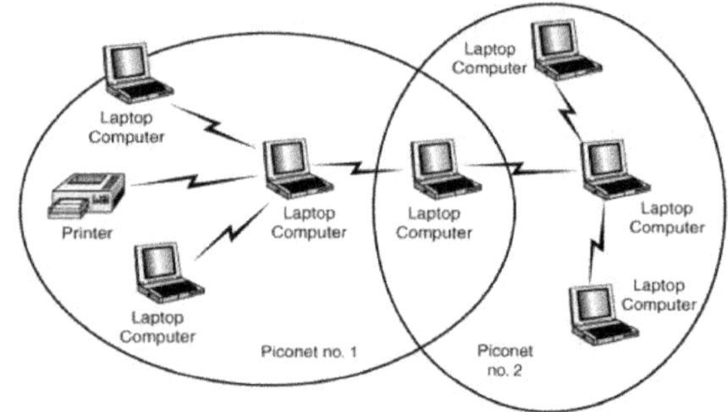

When different piconets are combined together in a way such that one serves as a primary station and another serves as a secondary station, what kind of network would be formed?

(A) Scatnet

(B) Dishnet

(C) Scatternet

(D) Segmentednet

22. Choose the port number of FTP.

(A) 23 (B) 21

(C) 10 (D) 25

23. What is the term used when the main server sends mail to another mail server?

(A) SMTP (B) FTP

(C) TCP (D) WWW

24. Identify the device used to boost up a weak signal.

(A) Modem (C) Switch

(B) Repeater (D) Router

25. Who keeps the private key in asymmetric key cryptography?

(A) Receiver

(B) Sender

(C) Both Sender and Receiver

(D) None

Darken Your Choice with HB Pencil

1.	Ⓐ Ⓑ Ⓒ Ⓓ	6.	Ⓐ Ⓑ Ⓒ Ⓓ	11.	Ⓐ Ⓑ Ⓒ Ⓓ	16.	Ⓐ Ⓑ Ⓒ Ⓓ	21.	Ⓐ Ⓑ Ⓒ Ⓓ
2.	Ⓐ Ⓑ Ⓒ Ⓓ	7.	Ⓐ Ⓑ Ⓒ Ⓓ	12.	Ⓐ Ⓑ Ⓒ Ⓓ	17.	Ⓐ Ⓑ Ⓒ Ⓓ	22.	Ⓐ Ⓑ Ⓒ Ⓓ
3.	Ⓐ Ⓑ Ⓒ Ⓓ	8.	Ⓐ Ⓑ Ⓒ Ⓓ	13.	Ⓐ Ⓑ Ⓒ Ⓓ	18.	Ⓐ Ⓑ Ⓒ Ⓓ	23.	Ⓐ Ⓑ Ⓒ Ⓓ
4.	Ⓐ Ⓑ Ⓒ Ⓓ	9.	Ⓐ Ⓑ Ⓒ Ⓓ	14.	Ⓐ Ⓑ Ⓒ Ⓓ	19.	Ⓐ Ⓑ Ⓒ Ⓓ	24.	Ⓐ Ⓑ Ⓒ Ⓓ
5.	Ⓐ Ⓑ Ⓒ Ⓓ	10.	Ⓐ Ⓑ Ⓒ Ⓓ	15.	Ⓐ Ⓑ Ⓒ Ⓓ	20.	Ⓐ Ⓑ Ⓒ Ⓓ	25.	Ⓐ Ⓑ Ⓒ Ⓓ

LATEST DEVELOPMENT IN 'IT' 

LEARNING OBJECTIVES

- ➤ Amoled
- ➤ PIM
- ➤ iPad Air

MULTIPLE CHOICE QUESTIONS

1. Apple iPad air runs on _______ operating system.
    - (A) Android
    - (B) iOS 7.0.4
    - (C) iOS 6
    - (D) iOS 6.4.5

2. Which of the latest version of Apple's immensely popular mobile smart phone released on September 16, 2022?
    - (A) iPhone 10
    - (B) iPhone 4
    - (C) iPhone 14
    - (D) iPhone 6

3. Identify the popular note-making software.

    - (A) Evernote
    - (B) NotePad
    - (C) Notice Board
    - (D) Note Taker

4. Which of the following is also known as a Recommendation Engine?
    - (A) Wikepedia
    - (B) Meta Crawler
    - (C) Google
    - (D) Stumble Upon

5. The Aakash tablet from Datawind runs on which operating system?
    - (A) iOS
    - (B) Windows Mobile
    - (C) Android
    - (D) Maebo

6. A series of e-book readers produced by Barner and Noble. Name them.
    - (A) Nook
    - (B) Kindle
    - (C) Cybook
    - (D) eDGe

7. Nexus 5 smartphone contains similarities of _______.
    - (A) LG G2
    - (B) Nokia Lumia 820
    - (C) Samsung Galaxy Core
    - (D) Samsung Wave 3

8. Arrange the android versions in ascending order (From earliest release to latest release)
    - (A) Donut, Cupcake, Éclair, Gingerbread, Froyo, Honeycomb, IceCream Sandwitch, Jelly Bean, Kitkat
    - (B) Cupcake, Donut, Éclair, Froyo, Ginger Bread, Honeycomb, Ice CreamSandwich, Jelly Bean, Kitkat

(C) Jelly Bean, Kitkat, Honeycomb, IceCream Sandwich, Froyo, Donut, Cupcake, Gingerbread, Éclair

(D) Donut, Eelair, Gingerbread, Froyo, Honeycomb, Ice Cream Sandwich, JellyBean, Kitkat

9. A personal cloud storage service is NOT provided by __________.
   (A) MediaFire
   (B) Google Nexus
   (C) Google Drive
   (D) Dropbox

10. AMOLED is a ______ for mobile devices.
    (A) Wireless technology
    (B) Touch technology
    (C) Display technology
    (D) None of these

11. The Xbox 360 successor which released on November 22, 2013 is __________.
    (A) Xbox 2010
    (B) Xbox One
    (C) Xbox 360S
    (D) Xbox 360 E

12. A PIM (Personal Information Management) application from Microsoft.
    (A) One Note   (B) Two Note
    (C) Sky Drive   (D) All of these

13. Mozilla launched a __________ version of its touch enable Firefox browser for Windows 8 and Windows 8.1 in February 2014.
    (A) Alpha   (B) Eama
    (C) Beta   (D) SIGMA

14. A touch screen device from Google that run's the company's Chrome OS.
    (A) Chromebook   (B) Retina Display
    (C) Surface Pro   (D) Nexus

15. Google Goggles was a downloadable image recognition application used for searches based on images taken by hand-held devices. They are examples of __________ technology.
    (A) Handheld
    (B) Wearable

(C) Real life
(D) Secret storage

16. A feature that enables Google Android-based smartphones, tablets and similar mobile devices to share content with other near-field communication-capable devices by simply touching the devices together and pressing a button on the device sending the content.
    (A) Android App
    (B) Android Launcher
    (C) Android Beam
    (D) Android wall

17. The smallest device in Apple's line up digital portable music players.
    (A) ipod Touch
    (B) iPod Nano
    (C) iPod Mini
    (D) iPod Shuffle

18. A supercomputer developed at Oak Ridge National Laboratory, funded by the U.S. Department of Energy which is capable of petaflops, or 20,000 trillion calculations per second.
    (A) iWarp
    (B) Mosaic
    (C) Titan
    (D) Titanic

19. A mobile commerce strategy that focuses on designing and developing e-commerce websites and related processes to improve the browsing and shopping experience on tablet devices.
    (A) Wi-Fi commerce
    (B) Tablet commerce
    (C) iCommerce
    (D) Mobile commerce

20. Samsung Galaxy Grand 2 runs on which of the following operating systems?
    (A) Android 4.2
    (B) Android 4.4
    (C) Android 4.3
    (D) iOS

21. _________ is Sony's name for digital rights management, a copy protection technology.
    - (A) Magic Gate
    - (B) Magic data
    - (C) Magic code
    - (D) Pro

22. An internet-based 3D virtual world where you move through the world as a 3D-Avatar is known as _______.
    - (A) Google-Maps
    - (B) Second-Life
    - (C) Del.icio.us
    - (D) Twitter

23. Pick the odd one out.
    - (A) **CARBONITE**
    - (B) BACKBLAZE
    - (C) CRASHPLAN
    - (D) twitter

24. SSL stands for _________________
    - (A) Secure Socket Layer
    - (B) Secure Secret Level
    - (C) Secure System Level
    - (D) Section Security Layer

25. Full form of W3C is _______________
    - (A) World Wide Websites community
    - (B) World Wide Web community
    - (C) World Wide Websites consortium
    - (D) World Wide Web consortium

Darken Your Choice with HB Pencil

1.	Ⓐ Ⓑ Ⓒ Ⓓ	6.	Ⓐ Ⓑ Ⓒ Ⓓ	11.	Ⓐ Ⓑ Ⓒ Ⓓ	16.	Ⓐ Ⓑ Ⓒ Ⓓ	21.	Ⓐ Ⓑ Ⓒ Ⓓ
2.	Ⓐ Ⓑ Ⓒ Ⓓ	7.	Ⓐ Ⓑ Ⓒ Ⓓ	12.	Ⓐ Ⓑ Ⓒ Ⓓ	17.	Ⓐ Ⓑ Ⓒ Ⓓ	22.	Ⓐ Ⓑ Ⓒ Ⓓ
3.	Ⓐ Ⓑ Ⓒ Ⓓ	8.	Ⓐ Ⓑ Ⓒ Ⓓ	13.	Ⓐ Ⓑ Ⓒ Ⓓ	18.	Ⓐ Ⓑ Ⓒ Ⓓ	23.	Ⓐ Ⓑ Ⓒ Ⓓ
4.	Ⓐ Ⓑ Ⓒ Ⓓ	9.	Ⓐ Ⓑ Ⓒ Ⓓ	14.	Ⓐ Ⓑ Ⓒ Ⓓ	19.	Ⓐ Ⓑ Ⓒ Ⓓ	24.	Ⓐ Ⓑ Ⓒ Ⓓ
5.	Ⓐ Ⓑ Ⓒ Ⓓ	10.	Ⓐ Ⓑ Ⓒ Ⓓ	15.	Ⓐ Ⓑ Ⓒ Ⓓ	20.	Ⓐ Ⓑ Ⓒ Ⓓ	25.	Ⓐ Ⓑ Ⓒ Ⓓ

LOGICAL REASONING

LEARNING OBJECTIVES

- ➤ Series
- ➤ Figure Pattern
- ➤ Figure Matrix

MULTIPLE CHOICE QUESTIONS

1. Complete the series _op _ mo _ n _ _ pnmop _
   - (A) mnpmon
   - (B) mpnmon
   - (C) mpnmop
   - (D) mnompn

2. Complete the series ba_ba_bac_acb_cbac
   - (A) aacb
   - (B) bbca
   - (C) ccba
   - (D) cbac

3. Complete the series m _ nm _ n _ an _ a _ ma _
   - (A) aamnan
   - (B) ammanm
   - (C) aammnn
   - (D) amammn

4. Complete the series adb_ac_da_cddcb_dbc_cbda
   - (A) bccba
   - (B) cbbaa
   - (C) ccbba
   - (D) bbcad

5. Complete the series bca_b_aabc _a_caa
   - (A) acab
   - (B) bcbb
   - (C) cbab
   - (D) ccab

6. Anthropology is related to Man in the same way as Anthology is related to
   - (A) Nature
   - (B) Trees
   - (C) Apes
   - (D) Poems

7. People is related to Chatter in the same way as Leaves is related to
   - (A) Whistle
   - (B) Ripple
   - (C) Rustle
   - (D) Cackle

8. Lion is related to Prowl in the same way as Bear is related to
   - (A) Frisk
   - (B) Lumber
   - (C) Stride
   - (D) Bound

9. Mirror is related to Reflection in the same way as Water is related to
   - (A) Conduction
   - (B) Dispersion
   - (C) Immersion
   - (D) Refraction

10. Firm is related to Flabby in the same way as Piquant is related to
    - (A) Bland
    - (B) Salty
    - (C) Pleasant
    - (D) Small

11. If GIVE is coded as 5137 and BAT is coded as 924. how is GATE written in that code?
    - (A) 5427
    - (B) 2547
    - (C) 5247
    - (D) 5724

12. If LUTE is written as MUTE and FATE is written as GATE, how is BLUE be written in that code?
    - (A) CLUE
    - (B) GLUE
    - (C) FLUE
    - (D) SLUE

OLYMPIAD WORKBOOK (NCO) CLASS– 5

13. If INSTITUTION is written as NOITUTITSNI, how is PERFECTION written in that code?
(A) NOICTEFREP
(B) NOITCEFERP
(C) NOITCEFREP
(D) NOITCEFPER

14. If GANTIC is written as GIGTANCI, how is MIRACLES written in that code?
(A) MIRLCAES
(B) MIRLACSE
(C) RIMCALSE
(D) RIMLCAES

15. If GOODNESS is written as HNPCODTR. How is GREATNESS written in that code?
(A) HQFZUODTR
(B) HQFZUMFRT
(C) HQFZSMFRT
(D) FSDBSODTR

16. Arrange the given words in alphabetical order and choose the one that comes first.
(A) Praise
(B) Practical
(C) Prank
(D) Prayer

17. Arrange the given words in alphabetical order and choose the one that comes first.
(A) Animate
(B) Animosity
(C) Anguish
(D) Ankle

18. Arrange the given words in alphabetical order and choose the one that comes first.
(A) Probe
(B) Proclaim
(C) Proceed
(D) Probate

19. Arrange the given words in alphabetical order and choose the one that comes first.
(A) Guarantee
(B) Group
(C) Grotesque
(D) Groan

20. Arrange the given words in alphabetical order and choose the one that comes first.
(A) Signature
(B) Sight
(C) Shrine
(D) Shrill

Direction (21-22): Dev, Kumar, Nilesh, Ankur and Pintu are standing facing North in a playground in positions as given below:
- Kumar is at 40 m to the right of Ankur.
- Dev is 60 m to the South of Kumar.
- Nilesh is at a distance of 25 m to the West of Ankur.
- Pintu is at a distance of 90 m to the North of Dev.

21. Who is in the North-East direction of the person who is to the left of Kumar?
(A) Dev   (B) Nilesh
(C) Ankur   (D) Pintu

22. If a boy started walking from Nilesh's position, met Ankur and then Kumar and Dev and then to Pintu. How much total distance did he cover while walking from one person to another?
(A) 215 m
(B) 155 m
(C) 245 m
(D) 185 m

Direction (23–25): Each of the following questions is based on the following information.
- Six flats on a floor in two rows facing North and South are allotted to P, Q, R, S, T and U.
- Q gets a North facing flat and is not next to S.
- S and U get diagonally opposite flats.

■ R next to U, gets a south facing flat and T gets North-facing flat.

23. If the flats of P and T are interchanged, then who's flat will be next to that of U?
(A) P (B) Q
(C) R (D) T

24. Which of the following combination gets the South-facing flats?
(A) QTS
(B) UPT
(C) URP
(D) Data is inadequate

25. The flats of which of the pair other than SU, is diagonally opposite to each other?
(A) QP
(B) QR
(C) PT
(D) TS

26. Choose the correct mirror image of the given figure (X) from amongst the four alternatives.

 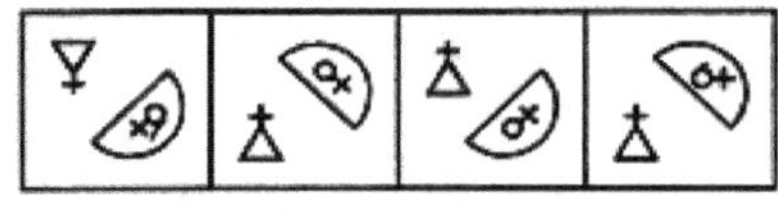

(X)   (1)   (2)   (3)   (4)
(A) 1
(B) 2
(C) 3
(D) 4

27. Choose the correct mirror image of the given figure (X) from amongst the four alternatives.

 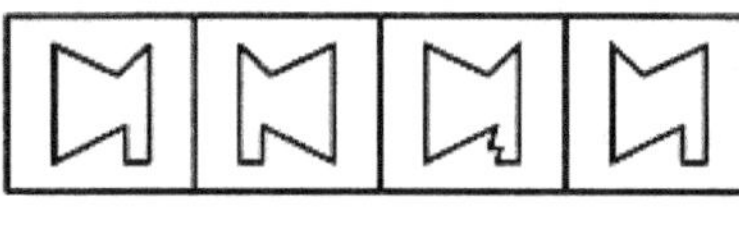

(X)   (1)   (2)   (3)   (4)
(A) 1   (B) 2
(C) 3   (D) 4

28. Choose the correct mirror image of the given figure (X) from amongst the four alternatives.

 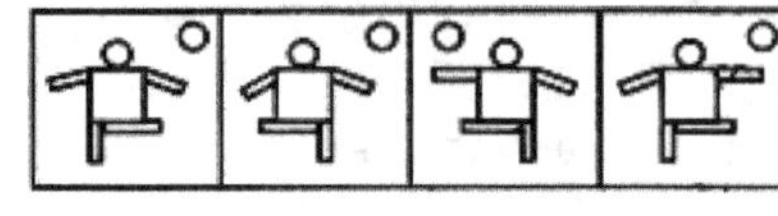

(X)   (1)   (2)   (3)   (4)
(A) 1   (B) 2
(C) 3   (D) 4

29. Choose the correct mirror image of the given figure (X) from amongst the four alternatives.

 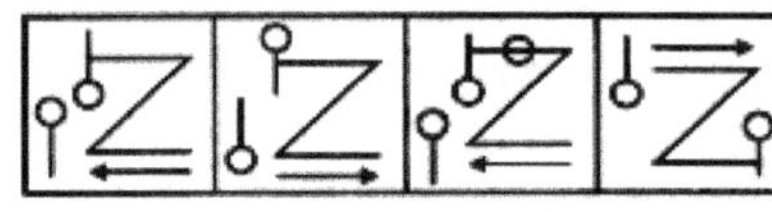

(X)   (1)   (2)   (3)   (4)
(A) 1   (B) 2
(C) 3   (D) 4

30. Choose the correct mirror image of the given figure (X) from amongst the four alternatives.

 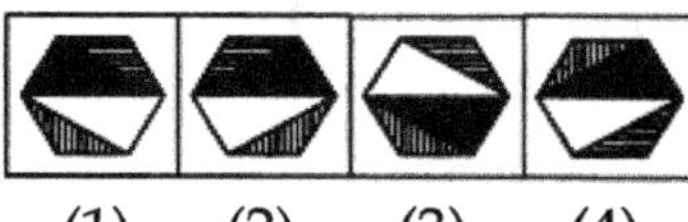

(X)   (1)   (2)   (3)   (4)
(A) 1
(B) 2
(C) 3
(D) 4

31. The angle 89° is:
(A) Acute
(B) Right
(C) Obtuse
(D) Reflex

32. The angle 234° is:
(A) Acute
(B) Obtuse
(C) Straight
(D) Reflex

33. The angle 98° is:
(A) Acute
(B) Right
(C) Obtuse
(D) Reflex

34. Which is closest to the size of angle AOB?

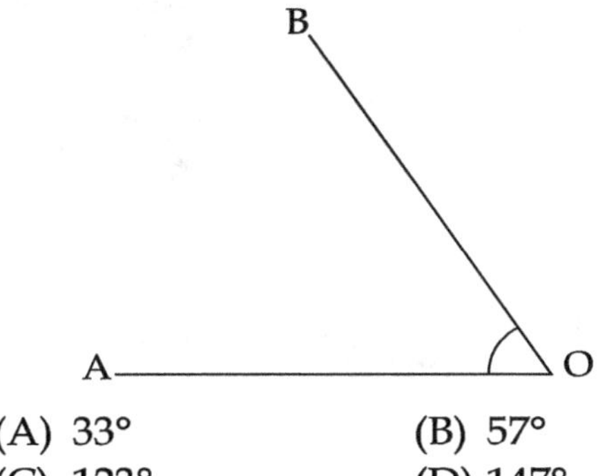

(A) 33°   (B) 57°
(C) 123°   (D) 147°

35. Which is closest to the size of angle COD?

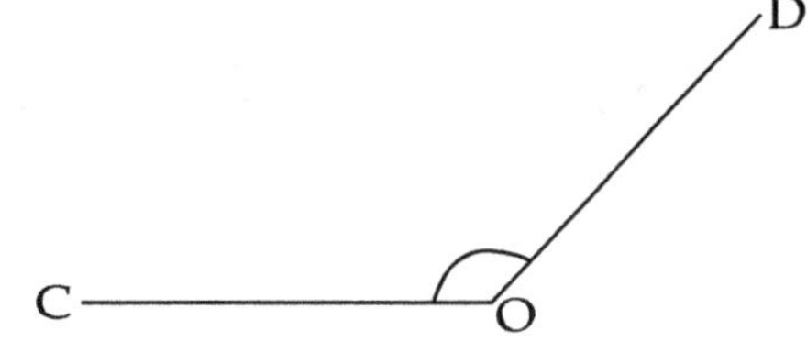

(A) 41°
(B) 49°
(C) 131°
(D) 169°

1.	Ⓐ Ⓑ Ⓒ Ⓓ	8.	Ⓐ Ⓑ Ⓒ Ⓓ	15.	Ⓐ Ⓑ Ⓒ Ⓓ	22.	Ⓐ Ⓑ Ⓒ Ⓓ	29.	Ⓐ Ⓑ Ⓒ Ⓓ
2.	Ⓐ Ⓑ Ⓒ Ⓓ	9.	Ⓐ Ⓑ Ⓒ Ⓓ	16.	Ⓐ Ⓑ Ⓒ Ⓓ	23.	Ⓐ Ⓑ Ⓒ Ⓓ	30.	Ⓐ Ⓑ Ⓒ Ⓓ
3.	Ⓐ Ⓑ Ⓒ Ⓓ	10.	Ⓐ Ⓑ Ⓒ Ⓓ	17.	Ⓐ Ⓑ Ⓒ Ⓓ	24.	Ⓐ Ⓑ Ⓒ Ⓓ	31.	Ⓐ Ⓑ Ⓒ Ⓓ
4.	Ⓐ Ⓑ Ⓒ Ⓓ	11.	Ⓐ Ⓑ Ⓒ Ⓓ	18.	Ⓐ Ⓑ Ⓒ Ⓓ	25.	Ⓐ Ⓑ Ⓒ Ⓓ	32.	Ⓐ Ⓑ Ⓒ Ⓓ
5.	Ⓐ Ⓑ Ⓒ Ⓓ	12.	Ⓐ Ⓑ Ⓒ Ⓓ	19.	Ⓐ Ⓑ Ⓒ Ⓓ	26.	Ⓐ Ⓑ Ⓒ Ⓓ	33.	Ⓐ Ⓑ Ⓒ Ⓓ
6.	Ⓐ Ⓑ Ⓒ Ⓓ	13.	Ⓐ Ⓑ Ⓒ Ⓓ	20.	Ⓐ Ⓑ Ⓒ Ⓓ	27.	Ⓐ Ⓑ Ⓒ Ⓓ	34.	Ⓐ Ⓑ Ⓒ Ⓓ
7.	Ⓐ Ⓑ Ⓒ Ⓓ	14.	Ⓐ Ⓑ Ⓒ Ⓓ	21.	Ⓐ Ⓑ Ⓒ Ⓓ	28.	Ⓐ Ⓑ Ⓒ Ⓓ	35.	Ⓐ Ⓑ Ⓒ Ⓓ

MODEL TEST PAPER

MULTIPLE CHOICE QUESTIONS

Mental Ability

1. The given bar graph shows the different kinds of vegetables sold.

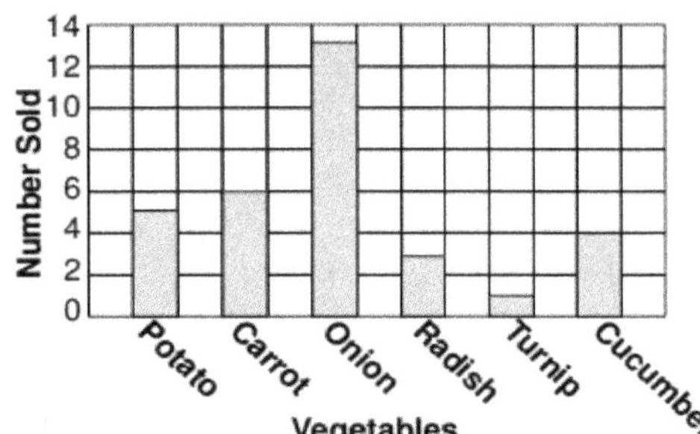

Which of these statements is false from the information in the graph?

(A) Fewer cucumbers were sold than onions.

(B) The same number of potatoes and carrots were sold.

(C) More onions were sold than all other vegetables.

(D) Turnips were sold the least.

2. In the cafeteria at a school, there are 8 tables for each grade. Which grade can have exactly 9 students sitting at each table?

Students in each grade at school	
Kindergarten	71
First Grade	64
Second Grade	81
Third Grade	63
Fourth Grade	80
Fifth Grade	72

(A) 1st Grade   (B) 2nd Grade

(C) 3rd Grade   (D) 5th Grade

3. On Saturday, 2,759 people went to the afternoon concert and 6,387 people went to the night concert. About how many people went to the concert on Saturday?

(A) 4,000   (B) 6,000

(C) 8,000   (D) 9,000

4. Which mixed fraction represents the shaded parts of the model?

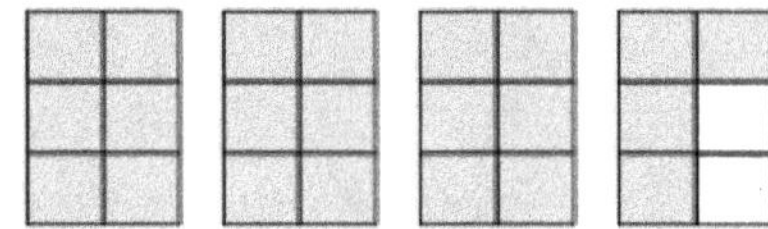

(A) $3\dfrac{2}{6}$ (B) $3\dfrac{4}{6}$

(C) $4\dfrac{2}{6}$ (D) $4\dfrac{4}{6}$

5. Mohit has 30 tokens to use on games at the video games parlour. For each game he plays, he uses the same number of tokens. If Mohit plays 5 different games, which number sentence could be used to show the number of tokens he can use on each game?

(A) $30 + 5$

(B) $30 - 5$

(C) 30×5

(D) $30 \div 5$

6. Which list contains only one prime number?

(A) 3, 4, 5, 6

(B) 6, 9, 10, 11

(C) 4, 10, 12, 21

(D) 7, 11, 13, 17

7. John drew a robot using only rectangles and hexagons. Which could be John's drawing?

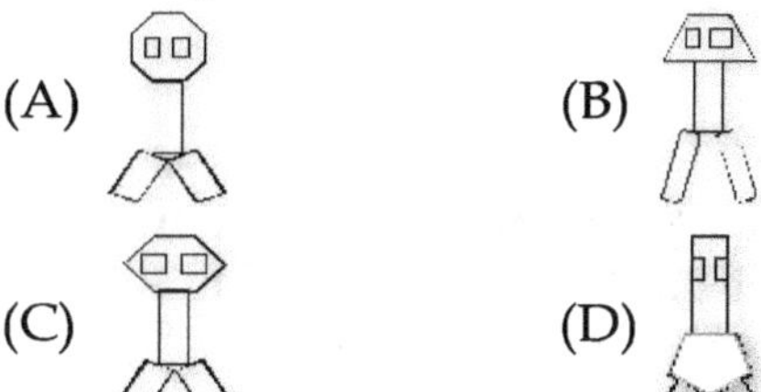

(A) (B)

(C) (D)

8. A drawing of Misha's garden is shown here.

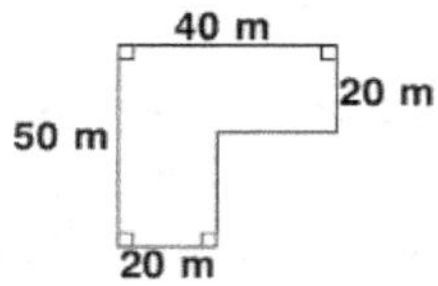

What is the perimeter of the garden?
(A) 130 m (B) 150 m
(C) 160 m (D) 180 m

9. The scale shown here is balanced. The bag of sand weighs 18 kg. Each of the cubes has the same weight. How many kg does one cube weigh?

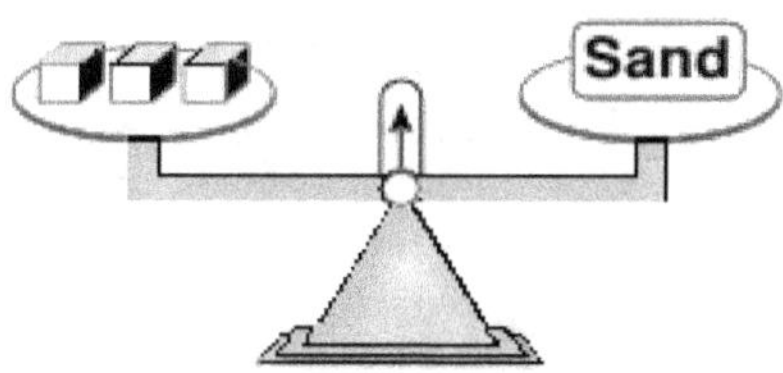

(A) 3 kg (B) 4 kg
(C) 5 kg (D) 6 kg

10. The given bar graph shows the average life span of some animals. Which animal has an average life span that is five times longer than the average life span of a polar bear?

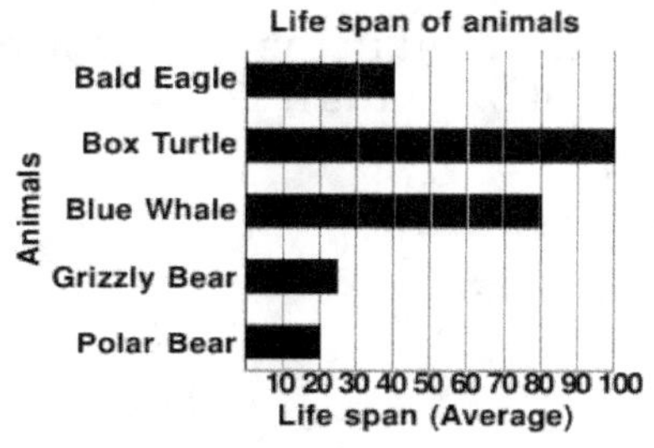

(A) Bald Eagle
(B) Box Turtle
(C) Blue Whale
(D) Grizzly Bear

Logical And Analytical Reasoning

11. The students at Maple Public School are selling flowers. Their goal is to sell 1500 flowers.

On the first day, the students sold 547 flowers.

On the second day, the students sold 655 flowers.

How many flowers must the students sell on the third day to meet their goal?
(A) 298 (B) 308
(C) 1202 (D) 2702

12. What is the value of $48 - 8 \times 4 - 6 \div 2$?
(A) 5 (B) 13
(C) 19 (D) 77

13. There are 20 red and 24 green pencils in a shop. The shopkeeper wants to distribute them equally in boxes. The largest number of pencils that can be put in each box is _____ .
(A) 4 (B) 6
(C) 12 (D) 8

14. Manali was making the house number board for her house using Roman numbers. Which of the following cannot be her house number board?
(A) VX (B) IXIV
(C) XIIV (D) None of these

15. Appu's school closed for summer vacations on April 26th and reopened on June 10th. Number of holidays are ___
(A) 46 (B) 45
(C) 44 (D) 47

16. If $\bigcirc + \triangle = 500$, $\bigcirc + \triangle + \triangle = 800$ then $\triangle - \bigcirc$ equals _____ .
(A) 900 (B) 100
(C) 300 (D) 700

17. Which is the heaviest ball?

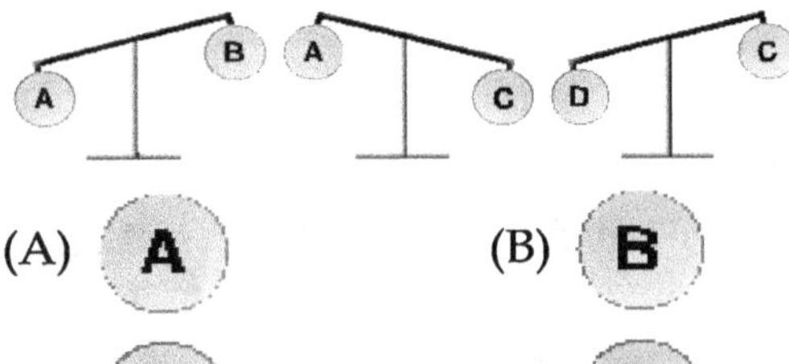

(A) 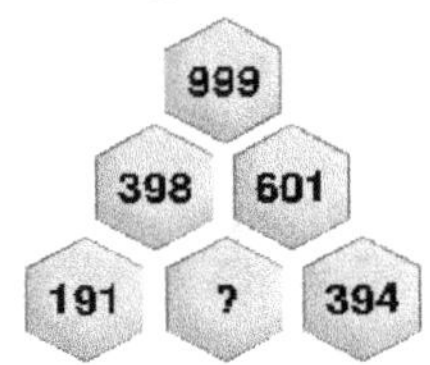 **A**

(B) **B**

(C) **C**

(D) **D**

18. Find the missing number.

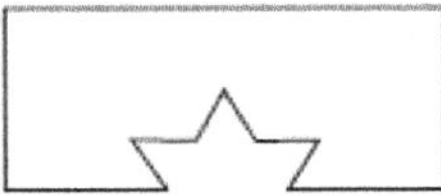

(A) 206 (B) 207
(C) 208 (D) 209

19. Sona folds a piece of paper and cuts as shown in the figure.

Which of the following will she get when she unfolds the paper?

(A) 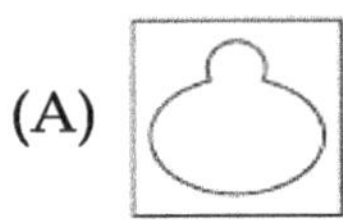

(B) 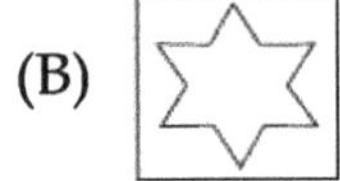

(C) 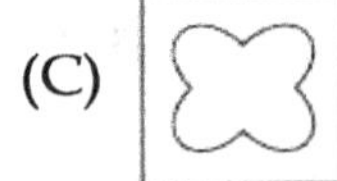

(D) 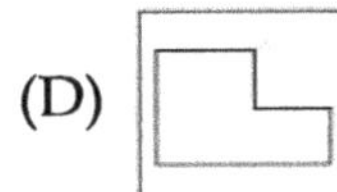

20. What is the mirror image of 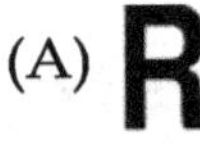 ?

(A) **R**

(B) 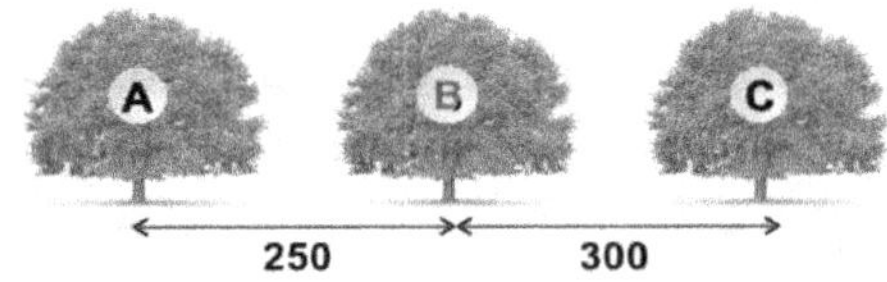

(C)

(D)

Computers & Information Technology

21. If "WHOLE" is coded as "LEHOW" then "MONEY" will be coded as _____ .
(A) EYNOM
(B) YEONM
(C) MEYON
(D) EYONM

22. Anusha cycled from Tree B to Tree C. She then cycled from Tree C to Tree A. How far did she cycle altogether?

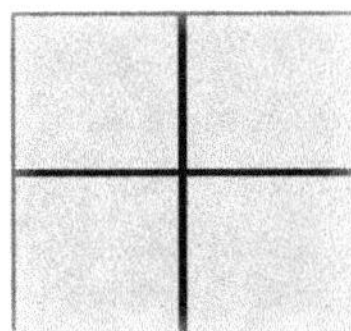

(A) 950
(B) 850
(C) 800
(D) 1050

23. How many squares are there in the given figure?

(A) 5
(B) 6
(C) 8
(D) 4

24. What is the digit in the one's place for the product of 5th Pattern 1?
Pattern 1 : 2
Pattern 2 : 2 × 2
Pattern 3 : 2 × 2 × 2
(A) 2   (B) 4
(C) 0   (D) 8

25. Samrat used a pattern for the given table. What rules did he use to go from the first number to the second and from the second number to the third?

First Number	Second Number	Third Number
12	4	7
10	2	5
15	7	10
17	9	12

(A) Add 8, subtract 3
(B) Add 8, add 3
(C) Subtract 8, subtract 3
(D) Subtract 8, add 3

26. Aryan used the number machine shown below to create output numbers from input numbers. The number machine used the same rule each time to create the output number.

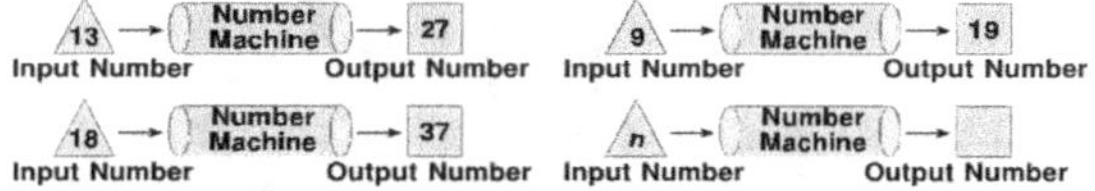

If n is the input number, which expression could be the rule the machine used to create each output number?

(A) 2n – 2
(B) 2n
(C) 2n – 1
(D) 2n + 1

27. On the map, each side of each grid square represents 1 kilometre. How much farther does Raj live from the Park than he lives from the Post Office?

Key

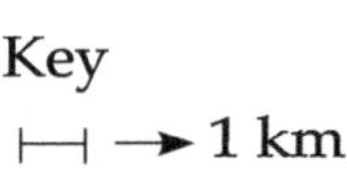 → 1 km

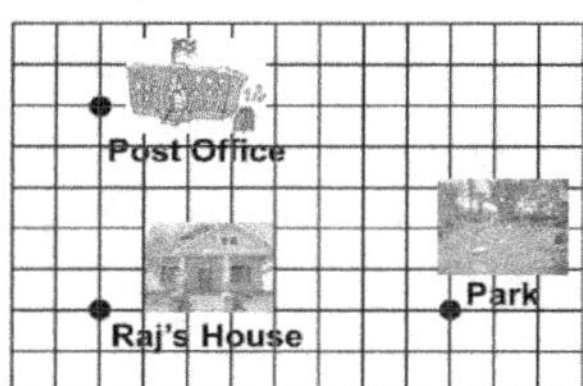

(A) 3 km
(B) 5 km
(C) 8 km
(D) 13 km

28. Mr. Abhay drew this pattern of shapes on the chalkboard. He asked his class to find the rule for his pattern. Which answer is correct?

  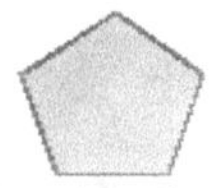 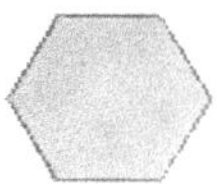

first   second   third   fourth

(A) All the figures have 1 less side each time first second third fourth.
(B) All the figures have 1 less angle each time.
(C) All the figures have 1 more acute angle each time.
(D) Number of sides is increased by 1 in the following figure than the previous figure.

29. Kartik has an apple, an orange and a banana. He is only allowed to have two for his snack. How many different combinations of 2 fruits could Kartik have for his snack?

(A) 2
(B) 3
(C) 6
(D) 9

30. Roy made the given pattern:

If the pattern continues, which shape will be in the last blank?

(A) ○

(B) ⊗

(C) △

(D) □

31. Meeku is setting up his new e-mail account. He needs to ensure privacy and security. Which of the following should he do?

(A) Pick a password used by another person.
(B) Use personal information for the new password.

   (C) Pick random letters for the new password.

   (D) Use a combination of words and numbers for the new password.

32. A network of computers and other devices that is confined to a related space is known as ______ .

   (A) Global Network

   (B) Local Area Network

   (C) Peer-to-peer Network

   (D) Metropolitan Network

33. A ______ is a website in which information is posted on a regular basis.

   (A) Forum

   (B) Blog

   (C) Browsing

   (D) Chatt

34. Multimedia is a combination of a few components, which are ______ .

   (A) Audio, video and animations

   (B) Coreldraw, MS-Access, Pag

   (C) Operating system, MS Word, Text effect

   (D) None of these

35. By default, your documents print in ______ mode.

   (A) Landscape

   (B) Portrait

   (C) Page setup

   (D) Print

36. Why can you not just start typing text on a blank PowerPoint slide?

   (A) You should use MS-Word if you want to type text.

   (B) The only way to add text is through the Auto content wizard.

   (C) You need to select the Autotext button.

   (D) You must draw a text box first

37. What is a slide-show in PowerPoint?

   (A) A special effect used in slide transitions.

   (B) A series of slides displayed in sequence.

   (C) The term for an individual slide in PowerPoint.

   (D) The button used to preview the slide you are currently working on.

38. Which of these mathematical expressions uses a superscript character?

$$6^3, \frac{1}{4}, 36\%, \sqrt{5}$$

   (A) 6^3

   (B) 1/4

   (C) 36%

   (D) 5

39. When viewing a video file, which button takes you to the final frame?

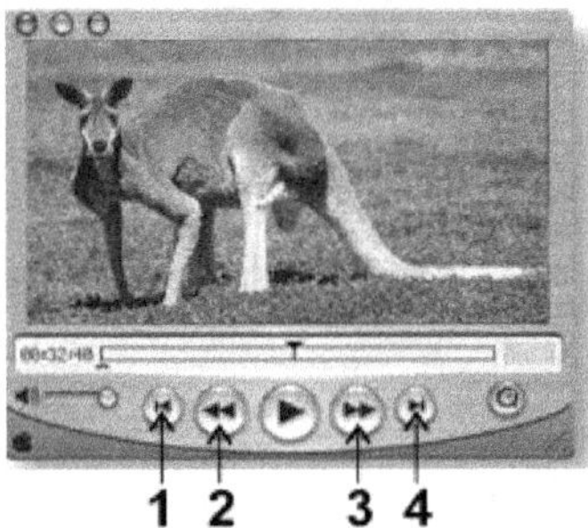

   (A) 1

   (B) 2

   (C) 3

   (D) 4

40. Multimedia is used in ______ .

   (A) Education

   (B) Advertising

   (C) Playing Games

   (D) All of these

41. Which device is used as the standard pointing device in a Graphical User Environment?

   (A) Keyboard

   (B) Mouse

   (C) Joystick

   (D) Track ball

42. Victor Middle School purchased a single-user copy of a word processing program. They may do which of the following?

OLYMPIAD WORKBOOK (NCO) CLASS— 5

(A) Copy it onto all the computers in the lab.

(B) Use it on only one computer in the lab.

(C) Use it on all the computers in the classroom.

(D) Duplicate the disk and give it to everyone in the class.

43. You have copied and pasted an image of a Tasmanian bird from the internet into a word processor document. Which handle should you drag to keep the image in the same proportions while re-sizing it?

(A) 1

(B) 2

(C) 3

(D) 4

44. Figure 1 was rotated to form Figure 2. Which handle in Figure 1 was used to rotate the image?

Figure 1   **Figure 2**

(A) 1

(B) 2

(C) 3

(D) 4

45. Your history assignment is over 30 pages long. You want to include the page number at the bottom of each page. What would be the best method to do this?

(A) Insert a reference line.

(B) Type in each page number.

(C) Insert the page number in the footer.

(D) Insert the page number in the header.

Achievers Section

46. You are sitting at a computer waiting for a web page to load but it seems to be taking much longer than usual. What could you do to load the page faster?

(A) Click the Back icon.

(B) Turn off the computer.

(C) Click the History icon.

(D) Click the Refresh/Reload icon.

47. The following is a file path taken from the footer in a document.

F:\SCIENCE MATERIALS\year 10\reactions.doc

What is the name of the file that has been accessed?

(A) F :

(B) year 10

(C) reactions.doc

(D) SCIENCE MATERIALS

48. You are on page 2 of a word-processing document of 100 pages. You open this dialogue box.

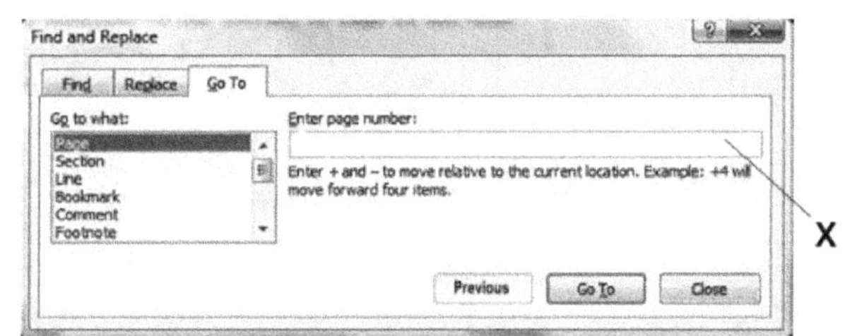

If you type '60' in the box labelled X, what will happen when you click 'OK'?

(A) A new section will be created on page 60.

(B) You will be taken to page 60.

(C) Page 60 will be deleted.

(D) Page 60 will be printed.

49. To open a disk, you position the mouse pointer on the disk icon, and then ___.

(A) Drag mouse while holding button down.

(B) Double click the mouse button.

(C) Roll mouse around.

(D) Roll and then click mouse.

50. You are about to compose an e-mail. Which section must be filled before the message can be sent?

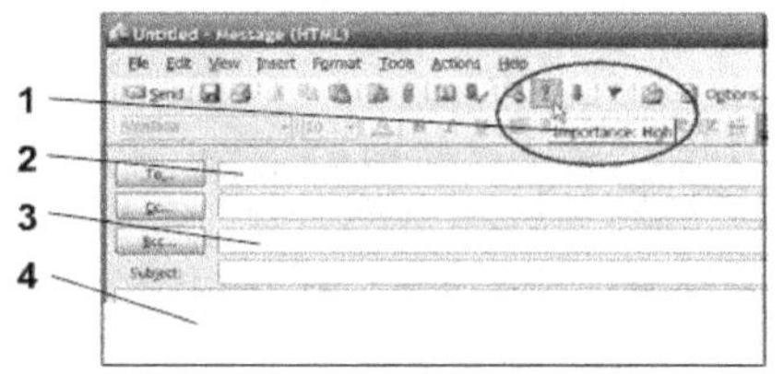

(A) 1   (B) 2

(C) 3   (D) 4

Darken Your Choice with HB Pencil

1.	Ⓐ Ⓑ Ⓒ Ⓓ	11.	Ⓐ Ⓑ Ⓒ Ⓓ	21.	Ⓐ Ⓑ Ⓒ Ⓓ	31.	Ⓐ Ⓑ Ⓒ Ⓓ	41.	Ⓐ Ⓑ Ⓒ Ⓓ
2.	Ⓐ Ⓑ Ⓒ Ⓓ	12.	Ⓐ Ⓑ Ⓒ Ⓓ	22.	Ⓐ Ⓑ Ⓒ Ⓓ	32.	Ⓐ Ⓑ Ⓒ Ⓓ	42.	Ⓐ Ⓑ Ⓒ Ⓓ
3.	Ⓐ Ⓑ Ⓒ Ⓓ	13.	Ⓐ Ⓑ Ⓒ Ⓓ	23.	Ⓐ Ⓑ Ⓒ Ⓓ	33.	Ⓐ Ⓑ Ⓒ Ⓓ	43.	Ⓐ Ⓑ Ⓒ Ⓓ
4.	Ⓐ Ⓑ Ⓒ Ⓓ	14.	Ⓐ Ⓑ Ⓒ Ⓓ	24.	Ⓐ Ⓑ Ⓒ Ⓓ	34.	Ⓐ Ⓑ Ⓒ Ⓓ	44.	Ⓐ Ⓑ Ⓒ Ⓓ
5.	Ⓐ Ⓑ Ⓒ Ⓓ	15.	Ⓐ Ⓑ Ⓒ Ⓓ	25.	Ⓐ Ⓑ Ⓒ Ⓓ	35.	Ⓐ Ⓑ Ⓒ Ⓓ	45.	Ⓐ Ⓑ Ⓒ Ⓓ
6.	Ⓐ Ⓑ Ⓒ Ⓓ	16.	Ⓐ Ⓑ Ⓒ Ⓓ	26.	Ⓐ Ⓑ Ⓒ Ⓓ	36.	Ⓐ Ⓑ Ⓒ Ⓓ	46.	Ⓐ Ⓑ Ⓒ Ⓓ
7.	Ⓐ Ⓑ Ⓒ Ⓓ	17.	Ⓐ Ⓑ Ⓒ Ⓓ	27.	Ⓐ Ⓑ Ⓒ Ⓓ	37.	Ⓐ Ⓑ Ⓒ Ⓓ	47.	Ⓐ Ⓑ Ⓒ Ⓓ
8.	Ⓐ Ⓑ Ⓒ Ⓓ	18.	Ⓐ Ⓑ Ⓒ Ⓓ	28.	Ⓐ Ⓑ Ⓒ Ⓓ	38.	Ⓐ Ⓑ Ⓒ Ⓓ	48.	Ⓐ Ⓑ Ⓒ Ⓓ
9.	Ⓐ Ⓑ Ⓒ Ⓓ	19.	Ⓐ Ⓑ Ⓒ Ⓓ	29.	Ⓐ Ⓑ Ⓒ Ⓓ	39.	Ⓐ Ⓑ Ⓒ Ⓓ	49.	Ⓐ Ⓑ Ⓒ Ⓓ
10.	Ⓐ Ⓑ Ⓒ Ⓓ	20.	Ⓐ Ⓑ Ⓒ Ⓓ	30.	Ⓐ Ⓑ Ⓒ Ⓓ	40.	Ⓐ Ⓑ Ⓒ Ⓓ	50.	Ⓐ Ⓑ Ⓒ Ⓓ

OLYMPIAD WORKBOOK (NCO) CLASS— 5

HINTS AND SOLUTIONS

1. FUNDAMENTALS OF COMPUTER

Answer Key

1. (B)	2. (A)	3. (D)	4. (A)	5. (D)	6. (C)	7. (D)	8. (D)	9. (B)	10. (C)
11. (A)	12. (B)	13. (D)	14. (A)	15. (A)	16. (C)	17. (B)	18. (B)	19. (C)	20. (C)

HOTS (ACHIEVERS SECTION)

21. (C)	22. (B)	23. (B)	24. (B)	25. (B)

2. COMPUTER MEMORY-PRIMARY AND SECONDARY MEMORY

Answer Key

1. (A)	2. (A)	3. (D)	4. (A)	5. (B)	6. (C)	7. (B)	8. (A)	9. (A)	10. (C)
11. (D)	12. (B)	13. (B)	14. (C)	15. (B)	16. (D)	17. (B)	18. (C)	19. (D)	20. (B)

HOTS (ACHIEVERS SECTION)

21. (B)	22. (B)	23. (D)	24. (D)	25. (A)

3. INTRODUCTION TO MULTIMEDIA

Answer Key

1. (D)	2. (C)	3. (A)	4. (C)	5. (C)	6. (C)	7. (B)	8. (B)	9. (D)	10. (A)
11. (D)	12. (C)	13. (C)	14. (C)	15. (B)	16. (C)	17. (B)	18. (A)	19. (B)	20. (B)

HOTS (ACHIEVERS SECTION)

21. (C)	22. (A)	23. (B)	24. (C)	25. (B)

4. WINDOWS 10

Answer Key

1. (B)	2. (C)	3. (C)	4. (C)	5. (C)	6. (D)	7. (C)	8. (D)	9. (A)	10. (C)
11. (D)	12. (D)	13. (D)	14. (B)	15. (D)	16. (B)	17. (D)	18. (A)	19. (C)	20. (B)

HOTS (ACHIEVERS SECTION)

21. (C)	22. (A)	23. (D)	24. (A)	25. (A)

5. MS PAINT

Answer Key

1. (A)	2. (A)	3. (B)	4. (B)	5. (B)	6. (A)	7. (D)	8. (C)	9. (B)	10. (B)
11. (D)	12. (D)	13. (D)	14. (D)	15. (A)	16. (D)	17. (A)	18. (D)	19. (C)	20. (C)

HOTS (ACHIEVERS SECTION)

21. (B)	22. (B)	23. (C)	24. (D)	25. (C)

6. MS WORD

Answer Key

1. (A)	2. (B)	3. (D)	4. (C)	5. (B)	6. (D)	7. (A)	8. (A)	9. (D)	10. (C)
11. (B)	12. (A)	13. (D)	14. (C)	15. (C)	16. (A)	17. (D)	18. (B)	19. (C)	20. (A)

HOTS (ACHIEVERS SECTION)

21. (B)	22. (D)	23. (A)	24. (B)	25. (C)

7. MS POWERPOINT

Answer Key

1. (D)	2. (A)	3. (C)	4. (C)	5. (C)	6. (B)	7. (B)	8. (B)	9. (B)	10. (A)
11. (A)	12. (C)	13. (C)	14. (C)	15. (D)	16. (D)	17. (D)	18. (B)	19. (C)	20. (B)

HOTS (ACHIEVERS SECTION)

21. (A)	22. (B)	23. (C)	24. (A)	25. (D)

Answer Key

1. (B)	2. (C)	3. (D)	4. (C)	5. (D)	6. (A)	7. (C)	8. (D)	9. (D)	10. (C)
11. (B)	12. (D)	13. (B)	14. (D)	15. (C)	16. (B)	17. (D)	18. (C)	19. (D)	20. (D)

HOTS (ACHIEVERS SECTION)

21. (D)	22. (A)	23. (C)	24. (B)	25. (A)

9. COMPUTER NETWORK

Answer Key

1. (D)	2. (C)	3. (D)	4. (D)	5. (D)	6. (B)	7. (D)	8. (D)	9. (A)	10. (D)
11. (A)	12. (C)	13. (C)	14. (D)	15. (A)	16. (B)	17. (B)	18. (C)	19. (A)	20. (A)

HOTS (ACHIEVERS SECTION)

21. (C)	22. (B)	23. (A)	24. (C)	25. (A)

10. LATEST DEVELOPMENTS IN 'IT'

Answer Key

1. (B)	2. (C)	3. (A)	4. (D)	5. (C)	6. (A)	7. (A)	8. (B)	9. (B)	10. (C)
11. (B)	12. (A)	13. (C)	14. (A)	15. (B)	16. (C)	17. (D)	18. (C)	19. (B)	20. (C)

HOTS (ACHIEVERS SECTION)

21. (A)	22. (B)	23. (D)	24. (A)	25. (D)

11. LOGICAL REASONING

Answer Key

1. (A)	2. (C)	3. (C)	4. (B)	5. (A)	6. (D)	7. (C)	8. (B)	9. (D)	10. (A)
11. (C)	12. (A)	13. (B)	14. (A)	15. (A)	16. (B)	17. (C)	18. (D)	19. (D)	20. (D)
21. (D)	22. (A)	23. (C)	24. (C)	15. (A)	26. (D)	27. (B)	28. (D)	29. (C)	30. (D)
31. (A)	32. (D)	33. (C)	34. (B)	35. (C)					

1. **(A)**

   The pattern 'mopn' is repeated.

2. **(C)**

   The series is bac/bac/bac/bac/bac/bac.
   The pattern bac is repeated.

3. **(C)**

   The series is man/man/man/man/man.
   The pattern 'man' is repeated.

4. **(B)**

   The series is

   adbcacbdabcddcbadbcacbda.

5. **(A)**

   The series is bcaa/bcaa/bcaa/bcaa. The
   pattern 'bcaa' is repeated.

6. **(D)**

   Anthropology deals with the study of
   man. Similarly, anthology deals with
   collection of poems.

7. **(C)**

   First is the noise produced by the second.

8. **(B)**

   Second is the manner of walking of the
   first.

9. **(D)**

   Light rays falling on a mirror undergo
   reflection and those falling on water
   undergo refraction.

10. **(A)**

    The words in each pair are antonyms of
    each other.

11. **(C)**

    G is coded as 5, A - 2 , T - 4, E - 7.

    So GATE = 5247

12. **(A)**

    The first letter of the word is moved one
    step forward to obtain the first letter of
    the code, while the other letters remain
    unaltered.

21. **(D)**

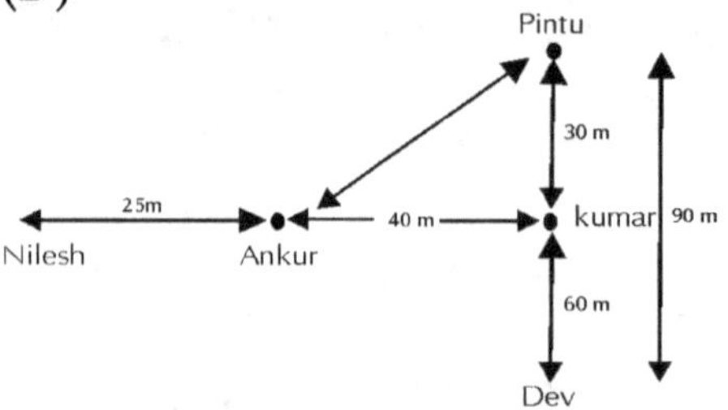

   Ankur is towards the left of Kumar.
   Hence Pintu is in North-East of Ankur.

22. **(A)**

   Required distance = 25 m + 40 m + 60 m +
   90 m

   Required distance = 215 m

23. **(C)**

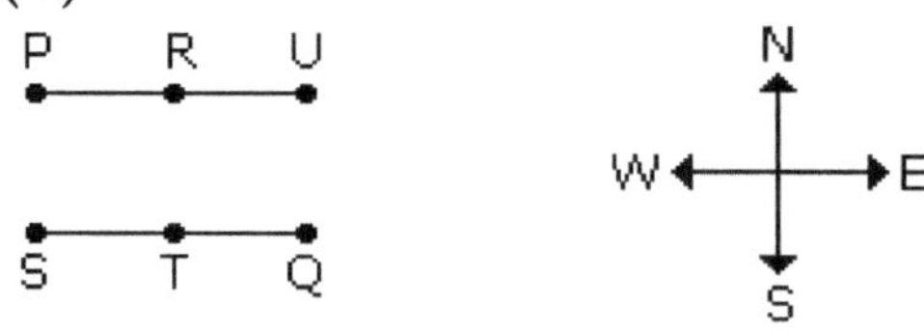

   Interchanging flats P and T

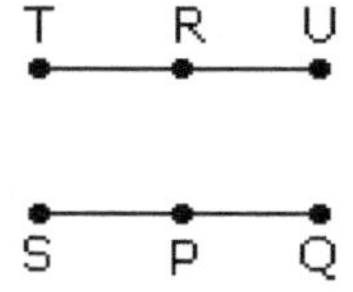

   Hence flat R will be next to U.

24. **(C)**

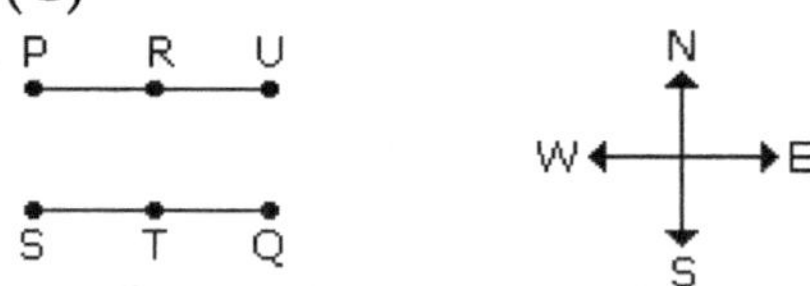

   Hence URP flat combination gets south-
   facing flats.

25. **(A)**

   Hence, Q and P are diagonally opposite
   to each other.

OLYMPIAD WORKBOOK (NCO) CLASS – 5

31. (A)

Since 89° is less than 90°, it is acute.

32. (D)

Since 234° is greater than 180°, it is reflex.

33. (C)

Since 98° is greater than 90° but less than 180°, it is obtuse

34. (B)

Measuring from O (Alphabet) in the direction of the arrow, angle AOB = 57°

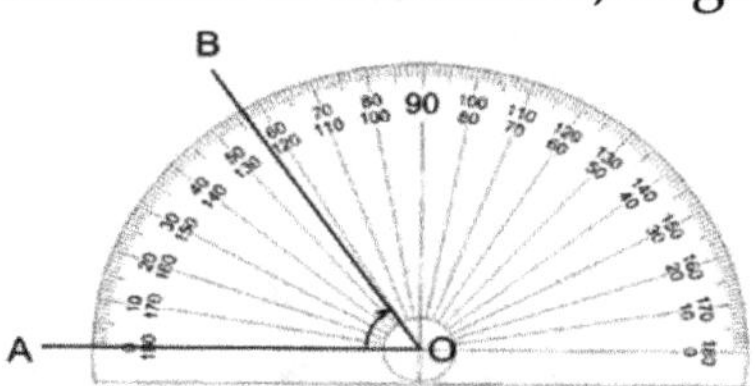

35. (C)

Starting from O, and measuring in the direction of the arrow, angle COD = 131°

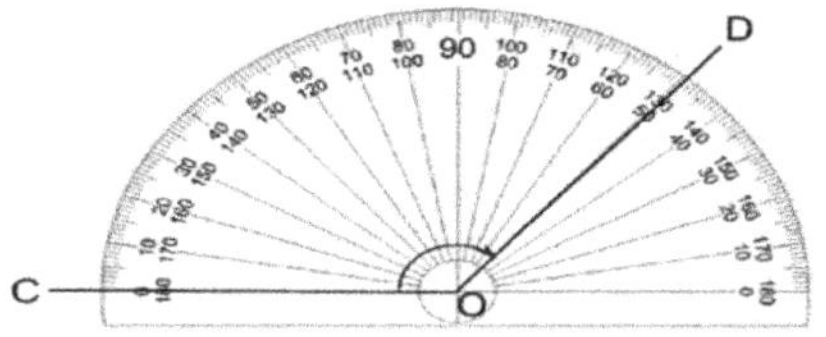

MODEL TEST PAPER

Answer Key

1. (B)	2. (D)	3. (D)	4. (B)	5. (D)	6. (B)	7. (C)	8. (D)	9. (D)	10. (B)
11. (A)	12. (B)	13. (A)	14. (D)	15. (B)	16. (B)	17. (D)	18. (B)	19. (B)	20. (C)
21. (D)	22. (B)	23. (A)	24. (A)	25. (D)	26. (D)	27. (A)	28. (D)	29. (B)	30. (B)
31. (D)	32. (B)	33. (B)	34. (A)	35. (B)	36. (D)	37. (B)	38. (A)	39. (D)	40. (D)
41. (B)	42. (B)	43. (C)	44. (A)	45. (C)	46. (D)	47. (C)	48. (B)	49. (B)	50. (B)

SAMPLE OMR ANSWER SHEET

1. STUDENT NAME (IN ENGLISH CAPITAL LETTERS ONLY)

Students must write and darken the respective circles completely using HB Pencil only. Othewise their Answer Sheets will not be evaluated.

PERSONAL DETAILS

2. SCHOOL CODE

3. CLASS

4. SECTION

5. ROLL NO.

6. QUESTION PAPER SET

A
B
C
D

7. MOBILE NUMBER

8. GENDER

MALE
FEMALE

9. STREAM

(Only for Class XI and XII Students)

MATHEMATICS
BIOLOGY
OTHERS

MARK YOUR ANSWERS

No.					No.				
1.	A	B	C	D	26.	A	B	C	D
2.	A	B	C	D	27.	A	B	C	D
3.	A	B	C	D	28.	A	B	C	D
4.	A	B	C	D	29.	A	B	C	D
5.	A	B	C	D	30.	A	B	C	D
6.	A	B	C	D	31.	A	B	C	D
7.	A	B	C	D	32.	A	B	C	D
8.	A	B	C	D	33.	A	B	C	D
9.	A	B	C	D	34.	A	B	C	D
10.	A	B	C	D	35.	A	B	C	D
11.	A	B	C	D	36.	A	B	C	D
12.	A	B	C	D	37.	A	B	C	D
13.	A	B	C	D	38.	A	B	C	D
14.	A	B	C	D	39.	A	B	C	D
15.	A	B	C	D	40.	A	B	C	D
16.	A	B	C	D	41.	A	B	C	D
17.	A	B	C	D	42.	A	B	C	D
18.	A	B	C	D	43.	A	B	C	D
19.	A	B	C	D	44.	A	B	C	D
20.	A	B	C	D	45.	A	B	C	D
21.	A	B	C	D	46.	A	B	C	D
22.	A	B	C	D	47.	A	B	C	D
23.	A	B	C	D	48.	A	B	C	D
24.	A	B	C	D	49.	A	B	C	D
25.	A	B	C	D	50.	A	B	C	D

Signature of the Student & Date of Examination

Signature of the Invigilator & Date of Examination

V&S Publishers, F-2/16 Ansari Road, Daryaganj, New Delhi-110002, ☎ 011-23240026-27
✉ info@vspublishers.com, ⊕ www.vspublishers.com